Down the Mississippi with Stinky

Down the Mississippi with Stinky

Two Women, a Canoe, and a Kitten

Dorie Brunner

PRAIRIE OAK PRESS
Madison, Wisconsin

First edition, first printing, 2000

Prairie Oak Press
821 Prospect Place
Madison, Wisconsin 53703

Typeset by Quick Quality Press, Madison, Wisconsin
Printed in the United States of America by Sheridan Books, Chelsea, Michigan

All photos by the author unless noted otherwise

Library of Congress Cataloging-in-Publication Data

Brunner, Dorie.
Down the Mississippi with Stinky : two women, a canoe, and a kitten / Dorie Brunner
    p.   cm.
ISBN 1-879483-69-6 (pbk. : alk. paper)
1. Mississippi River—Description and travel. 2. Brunner, Dorie—Journeys—Mississippi River. 3. Leidiger, Lou—Journeys—Mississippi River. 4. Canoes and canoeing—Mississippi River. 5. Women—Mississippi River—Biography. 6. Kittens—Mississippi River. I. Title.

F355 .B78 2000
917.704'33—dc21
                                   00-063718

*To all the misunderstood, abused,
abandoned, and lost kittens and
cats in this, their world, too*

Mississippi River Basin

CANADA

Minnesota

River's Source
Lake Itaska —— X

a

b

Lake Superior

Wisconsin

1

2

3

c

d

4

5

Lake
Michigan

Iowa

6

e

f

Illinois

7

Ohio

8

g

Missouri

h

9

Kentucky

Tennessee

Arkansas

10

i

Mississippi

j

k

Louisiana

l m

11

Gulf of Mexico

Major Cities

a. Bemidji, Minn.
b. Grand Rapids, Minn.
c. Twin Cities, Minn.
d. LaCrosse, Wis.
e. Dubuque, Iowa
f. Fort Madison, Iowa
g. St. Louis, Mo.
h. Cairo, Ill.
i. Memphis, Tenn.
j. Greenville, Miss.
k. Vicksburg, Miss.
l. Baton Rouge, La.
m. New Orleans, La.

Major Tributaries

1. Crow
2. St. Croix
3. Chippewa
4. Root
5. Wisconsin
6. Des Moines
7. Illinois
8. Missouri
9. Ohio
10. Arkansas
11. Red

CONTENTS

PREFACE

Forty years ago, my friend Lou Germann and I, both teachers in Wisconsin, decided to spend our summer vacation paddling down the Mississippi, 2,300 miles, in a canoe. This is the true story of our adventure.

I had often thought about writing a book to share our experience with others. Especially I wanted to tell about Stinky, a most unusual, loveable, and devoted kitten. He made our journey far different from the one we had anticipated.

Finally, after many years, with memories still very fresh and lots of time on my hands, I thought, "Nothing ventured, nothing gained." But the book probably would never have been written, had we not met Stinky. He was the main driving force. I wanted to share with others the story of this unique kitten's amazing and short life.

ACKNOWLEDGMENTS

To my parents, for their reluctant but unflagging support and encouragement.

Many thanks to Lou Leidiger, Las Vegas, Nevada, for agreeing to "do the river." Without her, this book would not have been possible. (It was the greatest adventure of my life and maybe hers, too.)

Thanks also to the following:

Bemidji Boat Company, Bemidji, Minnesota, for furnishing a worthy canoe and accessories, including a canoe motor mount.

Albert Ruesch, my uncle, for lending us the little 1-1/2 h.p. motor.

Heiggard's Tent and Awning, St. Louis Park, Minnesota, for supplying a very suitable tent, cots, and tarps.

Burton Motors, Minneapolis, Minnesota, for free use of a new Volvo while in the Twin Cities.

The JCs of Fort Madison, Iowa, and the George Alton family.

The JCs of Vicksburg, Mississippi, for supplying all our needs there.

The management and staff of the Sheraton Charles Hotel, New Orleans, Louisiana, for treating us like royalty.

Newspapers, TV stations, and radio stations along the length of river.

The U.S. Coast Guard.

Towboats and crews, especially the *Weatherwood*, Greenville, Mississippi.

Many people whose names we will never know, for their aid, counsel, concern, and support during our time on the river.

Bob Becker, Spooner, Wisconsin, for his advice and support in our endeavor.

My daughter, Sarah, of Barronett, Wisconsin, who has always been a boundless source of pride.

The Blue Hills Bookseller, Rice Lake, Wisconsin, and to Gail Waldron and Tammy Lundquist, co-owners.

Special appreciation to Sue Disbrow for her aid and interest.

Jill and Barbara Thomas of Medford, for their assistance.

Amy Lavin, of Medford, for computer help.

Maureen Conboy, Rice Lake, Wisconsin, for her encouragement and counsel.

My sister Marilyn and her husband, Don Ertl, for retrieving us from New Orleans and putting up with Stinky's antics, as well as our questionable appearance.

Prairie Oak Press, Madison, Wisconsin, and Jerry Minnich, publisher, for believing in my book. Jerry made the day for me, as well as a milestone in my life.

INTRODUCTION

The "Father of Waters" was named *Misisipi* by the Ojibwa (mis, "great;" isipi, "river"). Later the spelling was changed to Mississippi. The length of this great river can only be estimated due to its tortuous meandering in the South. The U.S. Department of Interior marks it as 2,348 miles. The greatest fall in the river is a drop of seven hundred feet in the five-hundred-mile stretch upstream from St. Paul, Minnesota. This great river will touch ten states before reaching the Gulf of Mexico. Because of its twisting and turning, and changing of course, it is a periodic problem for some states and counties. A resident who lives in a state or county one year, may find himself in a different one the year after. This is a frequent occurrence in the area of Tennessee, Kentucky, and Missouri.

The Missouri and the Ohio rivers are the two greatest tributaries, the Ohio being the larger. The Mississippi empties into the Gulf of Mexico at an average of 600,000 cubic feet of water per second. There are now thirty-seven locks and dams on the upper Mississippi. The first is at St. Anthony Falls, Minnesota, the last at North St. Louis, Missouri, a few miles south of the point where the Missouri River enters the Mississippi. The largest lock is at Keokuk, Iowa. It is 1,200 feet long, 38 feet deep, and holds 150 million gallons of water.

From St. Paul to New Orleans, most of the river has bank protection—levees, wing dams, and submerged devices, all in an attempt to control shifting currents, erosion, and flooding. Constant dredging in the South is necessary to keep the main river channels free of sandbars. Lighted buoy markers designate the river's safe passage channels. Mileage markers designate the number of miles traveled down or upstream. The U.S. Coast Guard patrols the river from St. Paul to the Gulf of Mexico.

From its headwaters to its mouth in the Gulf, the Mississippi is not only a great river, but one rich in history. It has played an important role in the making of America for hundreds of years. It is believed the Spaniard De Soto discovered the river in the South on May 21, 1541. He explored northeast into what is now Arkansas, and returned to what is now Louisiana, where he died in 1542 and was buried in the Mississippi. Other early explorations of the river further to the north were made by Joliet, LaSalle, Marquette, and countless trappers and traders, all with the help and guidance of the native Indian peoples. The entire river abounds with historical cities and sites. Because of the French and Spanish influence, many cities and towns carry French and Spanish names. Others carry the names of Native Americans, who had lived near or on the shores of the river for centuries before Europeans arrived.

CHAPTER 1

The Beginning

JUNE 4, 1960, WAS probably one of the most exciting days of my life. After almost a year of planning and preparation, my friend Lou Germann and I were finally ready to begin our odyssey down the "great river," the Father of Waters.

In early spring of 1960 we both had been offered teaching positions by the Shell Oil Company, in North Africa. We had a decision to make. We knew we couldn't do both Africa and the river. It had to be one or the other. The Mississippi won the vote.

Much of our spare time in the spring of 1960 was devoted to preparations for our trip. Since Lou was teaching in Rice Lake, Wisconsin, and I in Cumberland, only fourteen miles away, we could get together frequently.

The first order on the list was to gain an immunity to poison ivy. Somewhere we had heard that the banks of the Mississippi were heavily infested with this miserable, poisonous plant. We found this to be true in many areas along the banks of the river. In the past I had been infected many times, even when I had never been near the plant. Instead, I got it from my dog who had walked through it.

A doctor recommended "Aqua Ivy." It would take about three months of treatment with this drug (it was in pill form) to gain immunity for the summer and fall. Beginning in March, we began taking the pills. I do not recall how many we had to take each day, but I do remember as we approached June, the number lessened. Neither of us noticed any side effects from the drug. Best of all it did give us an immunity, as we were exposed to the plants many times. We walked in it—not because we wanted to, but because there was no other place to walk. On one occasion, we pitched our tent in a patch of it, as there was no other place at the chosen campsite to pitch it. This past year, I checked with several drug stores, and for some reason it is no longer available. In addition to the poison ivy pills, we each had a tetanus shot and a physical exam.

During the planning, we also had to find companies willing to donate a canoe and a tent. After several trips to the Twin Cities we found the companies to fill our needs. They in return received immense exposure of their products. When we canoed in Canada, we rented a canoe from a resort there. The tent we had was just a two-person army pup tent with no floor and no mosquito protection. Not exactly the ideal tent for an extended river trip. Even in Canada it never met our needs.

Now that we had the four most essential pieces of equipment—a canoe, two paddles, and a tent—we decided it was time to write some correspondence. We wrote to the Sheraton Charles Hotel in New Orleans and told them of our intention to canoe to New Orleans. We asked if they could reserve a room for us during the month of August. We couldn't specify a date, since we had no idea when we would arrive. We received a very positive response, saying that we were to be their "guests." Things were going well for us, and at this point in time we hadn't even wet a paddle. Several Junior Chamber of Commerce groups were contacted in cities and towns we would pass by.

We then contacted the U.S. Army Corps of Engineers, in Chicago. They could supply us with Mississippi River navigation charts from Minneapolis to Cairo. The charts from Cairo to New Orleans would have to be ordered from the Corps of Engineers at Vicksburg, Mississippi.

When speaking to a man in Vicksburg of our intention to canoe the river, he strongly advised we take a small outboard motor with us in case of accident, illness, or threatening weather. He also advised that we use it to maneuver through heavy river traffic when passing by or through large cities. The total cost for the two large maps (charts) came to $3.50. As I understand it, they are much more expensive now. The maps we received were dated 1958 and 1959, so both were a year or two old. In 1960, the main river channel, buoy markers, and submerged sandbars were not, in many cases, where they had been a year or two earlier. At times it was mind-boggling getting lost, grounded, and trying to figure where we were. The river's length is hardly ever the same, due to its changing course. *Encyclopedia Britannica* lists the river's total length as 2,348 miles. Since the river is constantly changing, no one ever knows its actual length at any given time.

From our summers canoeing in Canada, we had a pretty good idea of the kind of equipment and food to pack. My father welded quarter-inch round steel rods together to make a grill for us to use over a campfire. The legs of the grill were made to fold up. When in use there were brace rods to hold the legs in place. Along with this, he made an oven 12 x 10 inches, and 5 inches high. It also had legs that folded, which made the packing easier. The oven had one removable rack and a door with a latch on the front of the oven. The door had overlapping edges so that smoke and ashes could not enter the oven chamber. When we used the oven, we built a fire below and then placed some hot coals on the top of the oven. Periodically, small pieces of wood were added to the coals. In minutes we had fresh baked biscuits. The oven and grill were packed together in a tight-fitting, heavy-duty cardboard box. My father was an excellent welder. Both the grill and oven appeared to be store-bought. The grill was the same size as the oven, although the legs were longer.

All of our canned goods were just thrown into a medium-size gunny sack. It often weighed forty pounds or more, and at other times only a pound or two. I made a box out of wood, about 20 x 30 inches and 8 inches deep, with compartments for food which we had repacked into metal containers or glass jars. The cover was made of fiberboard, with hinges and a latch. When opened, the cover acted as a small table. On each end of the box there were rope handles for easy carrying. In this box we stored flour, sugar, rice, powdered eggs, potatoes, milk, etc. Although it contained mostly food and items for cooking, room was also found for soap and first-aid supplies, which included a snake bite kit. It also included a small metal box of nails of various sizes which we used numerous times but always tried to remove for future reuse. The nails came in handy when building a lean-to for shade.

We took candy, but never chocolate, which would just melt into a glob in the hot weather. For snacks, we brought mostly dried fruit, Kraft caramels, and jelly beans. Potato chips, crackers, and bread were never on the food list, since they would soon soak up the dampness and become moldy.

We had intended to begin at the source of the Mississippi, which is Lake Itasca. At the point where the river leaves the lake it is so narrow that one can usually jump or wade across it. In June of 1960, very little water was flowing out of the lake. There wasn't enough water to float a canoe, let alone paddle one that was loaded. So, as an alternative starting point, our journey was begun from the west shore of Lake Bemidji, which the Mississippi passes through. Strange as it may seem, Lake Itasca is about twenty miles SOUTH of Lake Bemidji. Therefore, the river flows straight north from the place of its birth. The Mississippi, being a river with a "mind or flow of its own," will continue an erratic, tortuous course another two thousand miles and more, to New Orleans, Louisiana.

As our red fiberglass canoe, compliments of the Bemidji Boat Company, was trucked to the lake, I still couldn't believe we would soon be on our way. Our parents were there to help us load the canoe and see us off. They had never been too enthused about our undertaking. We did write them as often as we could, and once in a great while were able to call, to let them know where we were and that we were both O.K. We never learned, until later, that they worried about us every day for more than two months. We never wrote or told them about the storms, tornadoes, serious mishaps, or even the unwanted visit by the mischievous "river rats"—all of which will be explained further in this book.

June 4, 1960, was an overcast and gloomy day. A slight drizzle began, which eventually became a steady rain. We quickly loaded all of our gear and supplies. We paid attention to balancing the load, but not to ready access of any particular item. It was shortly after noon when we left the shore of Lake Bemidji.

Within an hour we found that the packing of the canoe was a haphazard piece of work at best. When the drizzle began to change to a steady rain, neither of us knew where our ponchos were stored. After some frustrating digging, we finally found them. We also discovered that we had a small leak somewhere in the bottom of the canoe. This, I thought, is a great way to start a canoe trip. By four o'clock. we had reached the south end of the lake, where the Mississippi exits and again becomes a river. The water was very low, with most of the large rocks and deadheads exposed. The little water in the river was fast "white

4

water." It we dumped here, our gear and supplies could be lost and our dream would be over before it really began.

The power dam was closed and wouldn't be opened until the next day, for passage of the Boy Scout Canoe Derby. Shortly before we reached the power dam it stopped raining. Again, after looking over the river's outlet, we came to a decision that it would be wise for us to camp for the night and wait for the dam to be opened the next day. What time of day that would be, we didn't know. The first thing we did was gather wood for a fire. Most of all we wanted to get warmed up and dry. In not finding our ponchos soon enough we both had become wet and cold. The canoe and its contents could wait.

After we unloaded the canoe, we found two very small holes in the bottom. These were apparently caused by the top carriers used to transport the canoe to Lake Bemidji. We pitched the tent and made supper. It took us a while to pitch the tent, since we had never worked with this model before. After a few days of practiced teamwork, we were able get it up in less than ten minutes, and down in much less.

In the evening, we repaired the canoe. We had a good supply of fiberglass cloth, fiberglass, and hardener, all of which would be used on several occasions, and not only for the canoe. Had the canoe been aluminum, there would have been times when we wouldn't have been able to repair it. The first day's initiation on the river, or in a lake, was a whole day of learning. After a few days, we learned, by trial and error, where to pack our gear for balance, dryness, and accessibility. We had canoed Lake of the Woods, Canada, a number of times, but we didn't have nearly as much gear, since those were only three- or four-week trips. This journey was to be more than two months. Counting ourselves, the canoe held about six hundred pounds, which left us with five or six inches of freeboard.

Since we didn't know when the dam would be opened, we got up at the crack of dawn. After a hurried breakfast, we were washing dishes below the dam when suddenly the dam opened to let the Boy Scouts through. Dishes, tablewear, Lou, and I staged an impromptu journey downstream. We managed to retrieve most of our dishes, but again we spent the day drying out. Our clothing supply was very limited. We each had a Boy Scout knapsack which held the only clothes we would have for two months.

5

By the time we had our tent down and the canoe packed, most of the scout canoes had passed us by. Even though they were racing, they had it much easier than we did. Three paddlers to each *empty* canoe. When they reached their campsites, their leaders had already pitched their tents and made their supper.

From the dam we still had approximately ten miles to go in order to reach the southwest shore of Cass Lake, where the river enters the lake. After paddling and occasionally wading when the river was too shallow, we finally entered the lake. We could see the scout canoes crossing the lake, some of the laggards being towed by motor boats. At the time we thought that to be strange, since it was purported to be a race.

According to our highway road map, it appeared we had three to four miles of paddling to reach the southeast shore of Cass Lake, where the river continues southward. It was after six o'clock. Should we set up camp, or follow the scouts, who now were out of sight. With the canoe loaded to the brim, it would take about an hour and a half to reach our destination. We decided to take on the lake, even though it was late in the day. That decision was *one big mistake!*

CHAPTER 2

The Cass Lake Storm

FROM THE SOUTHWEST A light wind had sprung up. We thought nothing of it, except it was unusual for that time of day. The sky was overflowing with large puffy clouds, some of which began to take on the appearance of the birthing of "thunderheads." They should have been a warning that a storm was imminent.

We would be crossing the south end of the lake at an angle, northwest to southeast. After a half-hour on the lake, the light wind suddenly became a wind of great force. Looking to the southwest, the puffy clouds had become dark, heavy, rolling, newborn thunderheads, traveling at a fast pace right in our direction. It was far too late to return to shore. The whitecaps grew into great two- to three-foot chopping waves that threatened to swamp the canoe. On went the life jackets!! Next came a cold rain mixed with hail. The rain and hail mixture continued for most of the paddle across the lake. Still a good distance from the southeast shore, we were able to zigzag, making every effort to keep the stern or bow into the wind and waves, and still make headway. Every half dozen strokes of the paddle, one of us would stop just long enough to sponge water out of the canoe. In the noise of the storm, we had to yell at one another to be heard. In spite of the sponging, there was always about three inches of water in the canoe, which added more weight to the heavily loaded craft. Lightning flashed all around us frequently enough to give us light to see by. Looking at the lake, which we had to do, gave me the willies. Never in my life, before or since, had I seen so angry a lake. Black water, trimmed with huge whitecaps, seemed to go in all directions at once. We couldn't run or hide. All we could do was paddle, sponge water, and even duck our heads at a close lightning strike. Many of the ground strikes would light up the far shore, still some distance away. Had we been struck, we probably wouldn't have known what hit us. A lightning bolt, I have been told, travels 90,000 miles per second. Being struck by lightning was a distinct possibility. We were thankful the canoe was not *aluminum*.

It vaguely crossed my mind that we could very well be dumped after only two days on the river. We had been in storms on other canoe trips, but never at night and in the middle of a large lake. This night, lightning was our greatest fear. It would continue to be so for the next two months.

Just as we reached the southeast shore, the horrendous storm began to abate. To myself, I said, "Thank you Lord." We did it! Both of us were wet and cold despite of our ponchos. We felt and looked like two drowned rats. It was the second day of being wet and cold and another day of learning. It was now nearly 10 P.M. The scouts who were ahead of us were long gone. They must have known of the impending storm, which probably was the reason for towing the lagging canoes. By the light of a kerosene lantern and the moon, which we were glad to see, we pitched our tent and cooked our supper on a one-burner camp stove in the tent. We had a cup of hot coffee with a shot of brandy for dessert, providing both warmth and reward. Both of us were dog-tired from the tough lake crossing. It was one lousy day! We hoped tomorrow would be better. It wasn't long before we were sound asleep in our damp sleeping bags.

Chapter 3
The Swamp

THE NEXT MORNING, WE made the short portage around the Knutson Dam. Now we entered the Chippewa National Forest, one of the largest national forests in northern Minnesota. The river was fast, treacherous "white water," and we would have it the next several miles, all the way to Lake Winnibigosh. Because the elevation of the river had dropped considerably, it was like running a steep, narrow chute. It was fun as well as exhilarating, but at the same time scary.

After a swift cruise downriver, we entered Lake Winnibigosh, a very large lake. It's almost three times the size of Cass Lake, which we thought to be a big lake. It was a windy day, and having learned a lesson the day before, we hugged the southwest shore. As a consequence, it took all day to navigate Lake Winnibigosh, the last lake the Mississippi passed through in Northern Minnesota. Now, we thought, no more worrying about getting caught in an open lake during a storm. That night, we camped where the river flowed out of the lake.

The following morning, we entered an area of the river that was a total puzzle, one that wouldn't be solved during the entire day. Paddling water was plentiful, but we couldn't believe what we were seeing! Swamp and more swamp as far as we could see. Tall grass of some sort, growing six to eight feet high. We were completely surrounded by the grass and not one single tree in sight. There were small paths of water, hardly wider than the canoe, moving slowly in all directions. It was definitely "no man's land," or better said, "no man's swamp." It was hopeless to ascertain which water path was the Mississippi and which was a tributary stream. Although we had been warned about the tall grass and swampy area, this was far beyond our expectations. We were told to watch the grasses growing in the water.

If the grass bends, we would be in the main river current. To us, *all* the grass was bending! I didn't think we'd ever find the river, at least not this day.

Soon, the sun and heat began getting to us. The tall grass didn't allow a breath of a breeze to touch us. The swamp was a haven for hundreds of black flies and mosquitoes, which were a constant annoyance. One whole day went by and we still weren't sure whether we were in the main current. That night, since there wasn't one piece of solid ground on which to camp, we had a supper of cold beans and Spam in the canoe. Neither of us got much sleep.

The next day, emerging from the swamp by early afternoon, we at last found the true river. We camped for the night just north of Grand Rapids. How good it felt to be on terra firma once again. The tent seemed like a mansion, NO mosquitoes! This night we could sleep prone instead of half sitting up.

Chapter 4

Our New Companion

THE FOLLOWING AFTERNOON, A few miles south of the city, we heard a strange and mournful cry. We couldn't imagine what it could be. Then we heard it again, and this time it sounded like a catbird. But we weren't entirely sure it was. We stopped paddling and tried to locate where the cries were coming from. The cries became fainter as the current carried us downriver. Being the curious type, we just had to know what was crying and why, so we went back upriver to where we had first heard the cries. Then we heard it again. Whatever it was, we were very close to it.

Suddenly we saw what looked to be a small animal of sorts. It was stuck deep in a mud flat, and it was hard to determine what it was. As we moved closer, we found it to be a kitten! A very tiny kitten, barely alive. From its appearance, it must have been stuck in the mud for a day or more. We inched the canoe slowly onto the mud flat within reaching distance of the kitten. Lou, who was in the bow, was able to grasp the kitten by the nape of the neck and pull it free of the mud. We expected it to struggle and squirm, or even try to bite or scratch, but it was too weak to do anything except fall limp into her hands. It was the most miserable, bedraggled kitten we had ever seen. It was caked with black, stinky mud over most of its body. When Lou put it in the canoe, it just lay there, too tired and weak to attempt an escape.

A short distance downriver, we were able to beach the canoe on solid ground. With the kitten on the ground between us, the examination began. The kitten didn't show any fear of us and allowed us to look it over from nose to tail. Its entire head and ears were covered with fly and mosquito bites. Its eyes were nearly swollen shut, and there were numerous bites over the rest of its little body. It had every reason to cry!

After the mud was cleaned off the kitten and its eyes and bites treated, we could hardly believe that its fur turned out to be almost all white except for on its head, tail, and a small spot on its back, which were black-grey in color. We also discovered that it was a "boy kitten," which, if he lived, would grow up to become a tomcat. We guessed that he was about four weeks old. He couldn't have weighed even a pound, as he was mostly hair and bones. We knew he must be very hungry and would probably eat most anything. I broke a biscuit into small pieces, put a little jelly on them, and it took only moments for the kitten to eat it all. He still wanted more, but not knowing how long it had been since he had eaten, it was decided it would be best not to feed him too much at his first meal. After he had a drink of water, we made a place for him under the canoe tarp cover. For a short time he just sat there and looked around. Very likely he was trying to figure out where he was, and perhaps how he happened to be there. It wasn't long before he curled into a little ball and fell into a deep kitten nap. It was probably his first good sleep in a long time, as he slept until late afternoon.

As I watched him sleeping, it occurred to me that this was just a nondescript kitten with no pedigree. Not worth much, in the grand scheme of things. But, then, we didn't have pedigrees, either, so we might as well travel together. As the trip progressed, this little kitten proved that you don't need a pedigree to make your mark in life.

10

CHAPTER 5

The Naming

As WE PADDLED DOWNRIVER, it seemed that all we talked about was the little kitten. Where had he come from? Where was his mother? How did he get trapped in the mud? There were no farms near the river where we had found him. Surely a kitten four weeks old, the age we guessed him to be, could not have walked any great distance, especially through the swamps and forest land that bordered the river. The kitten had all the answers to our questions, but he would never reveal them. We could only surmise about his first four weeks of life. We believe he was born to a tame cat gone wild.

After a few hours of paddling, Lou suggested that the kitten should have a name. We each proposed several names such as—Tom, Buttons, Come'er, and others. There was a short pause while both of us were thinking of names, when Lou remarked that he was a stinky kitten when found. At that moment he was officially named "Stinky!"

So we talked into late afternoon, and it was all about Stinky. We were glad that we found him when we did. His life at the time was not measured in days or weeks, but rather hours. We wondered whether it would be wise to take him with us for the entire voyage. We still had about two thousand miles to go to reach our destination. Would he become a problem for us? Would he be able to survive the intense hot weather in the South? Being in a canoe all day wouldn't be very cool. We knew there might be times when we would be so involved in our own survival, we might not have time to look after a kitten. What would we do with him when making a portage? We had enough gear and supplies to carry without worrying about a kitten. Stinky slept through all of our kitten talk.

That evening when we pulled onto a nice grassy shore to camp for the night, we wondered whether Stinky would stay with us or run off at the first chance. After an all-afternoon nap he had regained an interest in the world around him. Much to our surprise, he stayed very close to our campsite. When we cooked supper over an open campfire, he made sure he wasn't to be left out. That evening, he probably had his first real meal in a number of days. After he had eaten, he just

11

sat and watched us prepare for the night. After the tent was put up and the sleeping bags unrolled, I noticed that he had fallen asleep—sitting up. I put him in the tent, and he made himself completely at home. Within minutes he was sound asleep on a sleeping bag. From that very first night he always slept in the tent with us. We placed a small box of sand in the tent, in case he would need it during the night. It was important to us that he be "tent broken." After a few days we discovered he never used it for the purpose intended. Instead he found it to be fun just digging in it. As a result we had sand where we didn't need it. The sandbox was eliminated as a tent accommodation.

CHAPTER 6

Stinky's First Swim

THE NEXT DAY WAS sunny and slightly warmer than the previous three. Stinky was lying on the bow of the canoe, his favorite spot, soaking up the sun. Having become weather-conscious, we kept our little transistor radio turned on for a weather report and maybe some news. The water was smooth but had a very strong current. As we rounded a sharp, narrow bend, we suddenly found ourselves heading quickly into fast-moving, boulder-strewn, whitewater rapids. If we hadn't had the radio on, we would have heard the rapids before seeing them. The next thing we knew, we were caught up in the rapids before we could retrieve Stinky from the bow. In only moments, there were but two of us in the canoe. Our "Commander in Chief" was in the river!

All we could see of him was his little head bobbing on the surface as he was swept downriver. It was obvious that he was swimming for his life. He was making every effort to keep his head above water. Suddenly he vanished! The swift current had sucked him under. I thought "That's the end of our Stinky!" But after a short period of time, which seemed like an eternity, he reappeared further downriver.

Both of yelled, "Swim, Stinky, swim!" I doubt very much that he knew what we were saying. I do think, however, that the sound of our voices gave him encouragement. He knew he wasn't abandoned. In our trying to avoid boulders, rocks, jammed logs, and river debris, it took some time to catch up to him. The rapids finally ended, but we were still in a strong current, and Stinky was still visible. He was obviously becoming very tired and wouldn't be afloat much longer. After some furious paddling, we finally caught up to him and fished him into the canoe. Stinky was just a small glob of fur with not much kitten under it, a very cold, waterlogged kitten inside as well as outside.

After a lot of coughing and sputtering, he was no worse for wear except for a few bruises. We towel-dried him and bundled him into a heavy sweatshirt. The rest of the day he spent sleeping UNDER the tarp. If he didn't learn anything else, he did learn how to swim without even one lesson. We also learned to never let him on the bow in rough or dangerous water. In spite of our caution, we fished him out of the river on numerous occasions throughout the voyage. I sometimes wondered if he fell in on purpose, just to cool off. It was not unusual for the temperatures to be over a hundred degrees in the South. It felt even hotter because of the ever-present humidity.

CHAPTER 7

Another Storm

EACH PASSING DAY BECAME slightly warmer. Stinky spent nearly every day on top of the tarp in the middle of the canoe or on the bow. The canvas tarp covered the canoe from stem to stern with openings only for the seating space.

We were unable to find a factory-made canoe cover, and so it was up to us to make our own. We took exact measurements of the canoe and finally found a store where we could buy real waterproof canvas. We spread it out on the sidewalk in front of my parents' home and measured and cut the canvas. Much to my mother's vexation, I sewed the tarp on her fairly new sewing machine. I must admit, the sewing machine got a real workout. But it did the job and survived without damage, except for many broken needles.

A good portion of the bow as well as the stern, was solid fiberglass. The tarp covering it made an ideal perch for Stinky. Kittens and cats like to lie or sit up high. The higher, the better to see.

Along the way, we saw many creatures of the surrounding wild areas—deer, beaver, mink, muskrat, fox, coyote, even a bear with her cubs, drinking at the river's edge. Leatherback turtles seemed to fascinate Stinky, as they made a splashing noise as they scooted off the mud flats into the river as we passed. The mud flats were a favorite place for them to sun themselves.

It was fascinating to see mother ducks guiding their young ducklings into hiding as we approached. They then swam off a short distance and performed an amazing act of fakery. They splashed and flopped in the water, acting as though they had a broken wing, to draw our attention away from their ducklings. The ducks were very wary of any intruders, and very protective of their young.

On this day, a storm moved in, a dandy "northeaster." A cold rain along with strong, erratic winds blew in from the north or east, sometimes from both directions at the same time. The trees along the riverbank gave us some protection from the winds. Heavy downpours of rain pelted us for nearly three days and two nights. When it wasn't a downpour, it was a continuous, cold drizzle. We couldn't camp and "sit it out" because we would then fall behind schedule in reaching the Twin Cities, where we had prearranged plans for the portaging of St. Anthony Falls.

Today it is no longer necessary to portage St. Anthony Falls, since there are two new locks there. Two additional locks have been added downriver. The Mississippi now has 31 locks in all, but when we made our voyage it had only 27.

The tarp protected our equipment and Stinky from direct rain. Even so, by the end of the second day it seemed that everything we had was either wet or very damp. When it rained, water would accumulate in the seats. We literally sat in a puddle of water every day, all day. We used large sponges to soak up the water in the seats and in the bottom of the canoe before it could reach our "Commander in Chief" and equipment.

Daytime temperatures were in the upper 40s. At night they would drop into the upper 30s, which was not unusual in northern Minnesota at that time of year. With the wind and cold rain, it felt much colder.

We believed that Stinky dealt with the storm better than we did. He never grumbled about the weather. Well into the third day, the sun let us know it still existed. Just seeing it break through the clouds lifted our spirits, and its warmth helped us dry out. By the evening of the third day we were able to build a fire for drying clothes and making supper. During the storm, our breakfasts and suppers were cooked in the tent on a small, one-unit Coleman gas stove.

If we had one thing to be thankful for, it was that we hadn't had another severe electrical storm like the one we had encountered on Cass Lake. Being on a large lake or even a river in a canoe during an electrical storm is fearsome.

CHAPTER 8

Stinky's First Portage

THE NEXT SEVERAL DAYS went well for all three of us. Stinky spent most of his time lying on top of the tarp in the middle of the canoe. Since I paddled the stern, I could keep on eye on him. But, we still wondered whether it would be wise to take him with us on the entire voyage. Maybe it might be better for him if we could find someone to adopt him. We made a couple half-hearted attempts, but found that we were becoming very attached to him, and he to us. Deep down in our hearts we really didn't want to give him up. He had added laughter to our sometimes tedious days. In the evenings he was full of energy after being confined to the canoe all day, except for a shore break at noon. He never cried or gave any indication that he was unhappy with us or his seventeen-foot-long home and playground. But we still wondered if it was wise for us to keep him.

A few miles north of Jacobson, Minnesota, we camped in a farmer's pasture that bordered the river. We could see the farm buildings about a quarter-mile away. Since we were nearly out of eggs, Lou was elected to find out if the farmer would sell us some. She was able to buy one dozen. Reluctantly, she then told the farmer of our finding a kitten and asked if he cared to give him a home. His answer was blunt and to the point. "I've got enough cats and kittens! I don't need or want any more!" Lou was as glad to give me the news of the farmer's refusal as I was to hear it. No more offers to anyone for a home for Stinky. We finally realized that he had the best home a kitten could have—WITH US!

We didn't get much sleep that night, with the cows and heifers milling around our tent. They even made attempts to chew on our tents' guy lines. It's likely they had never seen a tent before and were just trying to figure out what it was. When they left early in the morning, they left behind many piles of "calling cards." We were glad to leave this site as quickly as possible.

From the day we found Stinky, I don't believe he knew he was a kitten. Nor did he know how kittens were expected to behave. He broke nearly all rules of feline behavior, displaying very uncatlike preferences. In the evening when we would wade into the river to do dishes, and wash clothes and ourselves, Stinky was right there with us. He thought nothing of being in the water up to his knees and even his belly. He had no fear of water and didn't mind getting wet. It wasn't long before he would go wading on his own, chasing frogs and crayfish. He never caught any, but he never gave up trying. Very quickly he became a very special kitten. The thought of finding a home for him was the furthest thing from our minds. He had become a "river kitten" and seemed to enjoy every minute of it. He was nothing less than a very precocious kitten, which often times got him into trouble.

It wasn't but a few days after we decided to keep Stinky that we ran up against a real challenge. We had portaged several times before, but never with a kitten. It took more than one trip to move all our gear and supplies from one side of the portage to the other. It wasn't a long portage, only about a hundred yards. But it still wasn't practical to carry a kitten back and forth on each trip. We decided that we'd have to trust him and hope for the best. On the first trip, we took the items that he was familiar with: the canoe and our knapsacks. Stinky was put into a knapsack with only his head protruding. After an exhausting tramp along the riverbank, we reached the other side of the portage. Stinky made the portage like an old hand! We put him and the knapsacks in the canoe and anchored it in the river a few feet from shore. We just had to hope that he wouldn't jump out and try to follow us, as he had little fear of water. We left him sitting in the canoe.

We went back upriver to portage more gear, and when we returned from the second trip there he was, sitting on our knapsacks, looking for all the world like the "Commander in Chief" of the canoe. He had a look on his face that seemed to say, "Where have you been?" We still had to make a couple more trips, but each time we came back he was there waiting for us. From that day on, we knew he would never run off during a portage.

From northern Minnesota to the Twin Cities, we had to make about fourteen portages. Most were very short—spillways, (similar to very small dams), city dams, and log jams. Short or long, the canoe had to be emptied, or nearly so, and then repacked after each portage. We were able to do most of the portages without help. In some cases we could have used some help, but there was no one around within miles to aid us. Some portages were made with pickup trucks, and once with a semitrailer. We had camped near a residential area, I don't recall the name of the city. It might have been Brainard, Minn. We didn't begin taking notes of important happenings until we reached St. Paul. Then we wrote short notes of happenings on the river maps.

Ahead of us was a logjam of unknown size which we intended to portage the following morning. Shortly after we set up camp, some children who lived nearby spotted us. It wasn't long before some of the parents arrived, as well. In talking to them, we were told that the logjam was quite long and there wouldn't be any access to the river after passing the logjam for another ten or twelve miles. Now we were in a quandary!

Totally unexpected, the father of some of the children said he could portage us the next morning. We didn't know it then, but his truck turned out to be a semitrailer. Early the next morning, children and parents were at our camp to help carry all of our gear up a steep hill to the man's house. When I saw the huge semi we were to be portaged with, I thought, this could be a costly portage. Lou felt the same as I, but we had no choice. Everything was loaded into the trailer. It was then that he told us we could not ride in the trailer with our gear, nor

17

in the cab. He didn't have the necessary insurance for passengers. We would have to hitchhike.

We retrieved our knapsacks from the trailer. Room was made in mine for Stinky. As soon as the truck went down the highway to the designated portage, Lou and I began "thumbing" our way. In minutes a car stopped. One of the parents who had helped us load our gear decided to help us out. She knew the exact place where we were to meet the semi. She drove us down a dirt road toward the river. It was obvious that this portage site was used many times as it was very spacious, with ample room for the semi. The driver helped us unload all our stuff and pile it on the shore. I think he knew we could pack the canoe more easily without any help. By this time we had a specific place for each box, parcel, tent, sleeping bags, etc. Lou sort of held her breath when she asked how much we owned him for the portage. To our utter astonishment, he said, "three dollars would be fine!" We had expected it to be twenty dollars or more. We would later find that nearly everyone we met was eager to help us in any way possible.

With each mile, the river became wider as we proceeded toward the Twin Cities. We also began to see more farms near the river. The heavy forestland, large lake paddling, and remoteness were behind us. The river no longer moved in a winding course as it had further north. For the first time, we could see what was ahead of us for quite a distance.

Looking far downriver, we spotted two large, black objects on a mudflat. Initially we thought they might be two large oil or gas drums. Or maybe two large logs embedded in the muck from the spring flooding. Soon we detected a strong stench of something decaying. As we got closer we saw, to our dismay, two large Holstein dairy cows stuck in the muck right up to their stomachs. They were dead! They looked as if they could explode at any time from the gases of decay. The suction of the muck held them up on all four legs. The sight was so overwhelming it even woke Stinky, who was sleeping at the time. It took us a few days to get over the cow incident. Our thoughts were with Stinky, and how he could have died in the muck like the cows. He was lucky that we found him in time. We never saw any wild animals trapped in the muck. Their wild instinct warned them of the danger.

18

CHAPTER 9

The Twin Cities

As we neared the Twin Cities, we were seeing and meeting more people on the river and in the small towns and cities near the river. Stinky made his presence known to everyone. Some folks couldn't believe their eyes. A *kitten* lying on the bow of a canoe? Others thought he was a stuffed kitten that we had placed there as a figurehead, like the Vikings had on the prows of their ships. Many people couldn't imagine our taking a kitten to New Orleans in a canoe. Everyone knew our destination without asking. Our origin (Bemidji, Minn.) and destination (New Orleans, La.) were painted on both sides of the canoe. Many wanted to know all about Stinky, and why we had him with us. The story of our finding and rescuing him was told many times over before we reached New Orleans. There were many, especially children, who wanted Stinky for their own. Days earlier, we might have considered giving him to someone. But not any more. Stinky had become too much a part of our life on the river. In time, he would play a significant part in the success of our voyage.

We arrived at our designated portage point in North Minneapolis right on time. Portaging St. Anthony Falls by pickup truck was a new experience for Stinky. He was a little fearful for the first few minutes, probably because of the noise of the truck and the city traffic. He later settled in, however, and appeared to enjoy the ride. I know Lou and I did. It was our very last portage. From that point on we would go through the locks and dams like all the other watercraft. There were times when the locks had to be filled or emptied just for our lone canoe. After we left the Twin Cities, we saw no other canoes on the river.

By late morning, our portage was completed at a site just north of the St. Paul Yacht Club. There we met with our parents who had brought additional equipment. We replaced the cold-weather sleeping bags with cots and one blanket each. We exchanged our heavier clothing for lightweight summer garb. (There were to be several times during the next week or two when we wished for warmer clothing and more than one blanket.) The Corps of Engineers recommended we have some motor power in the event of an accident, illness, or severe weather, so we added a little one and one-half horsepower motor. As it turned out, we used it more than we had expected.

Early in the afternoon, a newspaper reporter showed up, the first of many to come. We were interviewed and pictures were taken. Stinky, of course, was included. As we moved downriver, just about everyone knew about Stinky, before they even saw him.

We drove a Volvo lent to us by Borton Motors to a grocery store to stock up on food. We didn't know when we would be able to shop again. But there was also a limit on the amount, because of the weight and space available in the canoe. Our purchases consisted primarily of canned meat, vegetables, fresh and dried fruit, stews, coffee, packaged soups, spaghetti, rice, powdered eggs, milk, and potatoes. Bisquick was a must. Bread was too bulky and usually turned moldy in a few days.

We baked biscuits in the small oven over a campfire. We included a small bag of dry cat food for Stinky. From the day we found him, he had been sharing our food. We had a small cooler, but rarely any ice to keep leftovers cold. After we found Stinky, he became our "leftover container!" Two of his favorite meals were Italian spaghetti and Spam with green beans.

CHAPTER 10

The Cruiser's Rescue

LATE IN THE AFTERNOON, we loaded the canoe to leave St. Paul. We wanted to be out of the city by nightfall so we could find a place to camp. We had paddled only about half an hour and were nearing the Yacht Club when the weather suddenly turned nasty. Out came the little radio. Tornado warnings were out! The wind increased in force, along with a deluge of rain mixed with heavy hail the size of large marbles. Stinky quickly dove under the tarp. Hail was not his cup of tea! We knew we had to head for shore and seek shelter. The only place was the Yacht Club. All of the slips had roofs, and we found one that was empty. We were safe and out of the weather for the moment and hoped the tornado would pass us by.

As we sat there assessing our predicament, a ferocious storm was tearing across the river, a river we could barely see because of the heavy hail, rain, and wind. Our plan to find a place to camp for the night was crushed.

The next thing we knew, a very large cabin cruiser approached the slip that we had parked in. Hastily, we unloaded the canoe onto the walkway which had no roof. Most of our equipment was covered with the tarp. I had Stinky tucked inside my poncho, but being a very nosey kitten, he just had to have his head out to see what was going on. The hail had stopped but it was still pouring buckets of rain.

As we sat there watching the cruiser enter the slip, we again talked of where we would spend the night. If it quit raining, we could sleep on the walkway without a tent. It was much too late to look for a camp-site. We also wondered whether the owner of the cruiser would be angry with us. We had no legal right to enter his rented slip. While pondering our plight, the owner of the cruiser walked toward us with a big grin on his face. We couldn't figure out what he thought was so funny! It turned out that he was grinning because of our appearance. We looked and felt like three drowned rats sitting among our gear. At first glance he, too, thought Stinky was a stuffed kitten. He appeared to be a very nice man, a real gentleman. In this case, appearance didn't lie. With a bigger grin on his face, he said that we could spend the night on his cruiser if we cared to. If we cared to? He had to be kidding!! We couldn't believe our ears and good fortune. What a generous offer from someone we had met only minutes before. The offer was readily accepted. How lucky could we get?

He helped us take aboard the things we would need for the night. There was a galley where we could cook, and all the necessities of home, including electric lights, bunks to sleep in, and chairs to sit on. We felt like we were in a palace, after many days of doing without these civilized comforts. We just couldn't imagine that the man would offer accommodations such as these to two total strangers and a kitten.

After we were all settled in, he said he would be back later in the evening and he would bring his wife so she could meet Stinky and us. It had stopped raining. The sun peeked through the thinning clouds, and then we knew the storm had passed. Stinky too, must have known the storm was over, for he walked to the cabin door to be let out. This was a real surprise for us. He had never been in a building or any craft other than the canoe. Lou carried him to shore, and he did "his thing." From then on, no matter where he was, we knew we would never be embarrassed by Stinky. He was one smart kitten, becoming a cat.

When the man returned in the evening with his wife, they first had to hear all about Stinky and how we came to have him with us. Stinky sat on the lady's lap enjoying all the special attention he was receiving. Lou and I couldn't find the words to express our gratitude for their generosity and kindness. This man and his wife were two of the many, many people who offered assistance and advice on our way down the great river.

After the couple left, we prepared for bed. All three of us had had a long day, especially Stinky. He hadn't had a kitten nap all day, and it wasn't long before he fell sound asleep and never woke until morning.

CHAPTER 11

Our First Lock

THE FOLLOWING MORNING, WE were up early to be on our way. We locked the cruiser and hid the key at an appointed place. As we paddled out onto the river, on the second leg of our journey, boats of all sizes could be seen. But, no canoes. There were a lot of towboats pushing barges which we had to stay clear of, as their prop-wash could suck the canoe toward them if we got too close.

This day we put Stinky in the middle of the canoe on top of the tarp. Because of all the boat traffic the river was very rough and choppy. Now was not the time to have a kitten in the river. This was a whole new experience for Lou and me. We had never paddled in so much river traffic before. Clearly, we were novices and had much to learn—and learn we did!

Until the first day out of St. Paul, we had used Minnesota road maps to follow the river. Now we would begin using the first of two Corps of Engineer river maps, which were in a bound tablet form. The first would take us from St. Paul, Minnesota, to Cairo, Illinois, a total of 840 miles and 27 locks. The last lock was in St. Louis, just a few miles south of the point where the Missouri River enters the Mississippi.

We were told that the most rigorous part of the river to canoe would be from the headwaters to the Twin Cities. It was difficult because of the many portages, shallow and steep rapids, and the cold and rain. The remoteness of the river was an added danger. We had the company of black flies during the day and mosquitoes at night. The river water was reasonably clean. We could use it for cooking, washing clothes, and mess kits. We drank it, too, after treating it with water purification tablets. After a whole day on the river, we could take a swim in the evening. The upper Mississippi was both good and bad to us, a very adventurous 495 miles.

After leaving St. Paul we found some of the less attractive parts of the river were yet to come. The river would test all three of us on our physical and mental endurance, and the sturdiness of our little ninety-pound, seventeen-foot canoe. Mother Nature would confront us on numerous occasions. The heat was frequently over a hundred and there was often no shade. There were sand fleas and the ever-present mosquitoes. From now on, we would also have to be on the watch for rattlesnakes and the deadly water moccasin, which is sometimes called the cottonmouth.

Erratic currents caused submerged trees and parts of trees from the spring floods to suddenly pop up out of the water and slowly be sucked back down out of sight. When the currents pulled them up, they came shooting out of the water with great force and could easily damage any craft smaller than a towboat or ship, or even sink it. This debris was most common around Prescott, Wisconsin, and on down into Iowa. The Corps of Engineers keeps the main river channel navigable and free of debris and sandbars by constant dredging year-round in the South, and spring through fall in the north. The channel is marked by large buoys from the Twin Cities to the Gulf of Mexico. It is never the same from year to year, because of the meandering of the river. The very first day out of St. Paul we found that if we got too close to the buoys, the current would suck us right into them. Since we were in a little canoe, we couldn't always stay in the main channel because of heavy river traffic or rough weather.

Most of the time we knew where we were, in spite of the one- and two-year-old maps. The navigation lines shown on the first map indicated the location of the navigation channels in the spring of 1953, seven years before our voyage. The first map book (charts) took us from St. Paul, Minnesota, to Cairo, Illinois. It was quite different from the second map book, which would take us from Cairo to New Orleans. The first map book, "The Upper Mississippi," had the mileage marked in segmented red lines with a + sign at the beginning and end of each line. These red lines indicated the river's navigation channel for large boat and barge traffic. Each group of these segmented lines represented one mile. After each five miles the total number of miles traveled was printed. There were also mileage posts on the river's shore, much like the Alcan Highway in Alaska. Luckily we had added a pair of binoculars to our gear list. They were put into use very nearly every day to locate the sign posts as well as government lights and day markers on shore. In addition there were lighted and unlighted buoy markers which, with the binoculars, we could see far ahead of us. The locations of navigation signs are changed from time to time. The first book was a little confusing at times because we had to begin at the last page and continued on to the first. The second book of maps, from Cairo to the Gulf of Mexico was read from the first page to the last. It was also different in other ways from the first book.

The red navigation lines were solid, not segmented, with a red 0 at the end of each line. At each five-mile marker the number of miles remaining to reach the Gulf of Mexico was printed in red. Since New Orleans is ninety-one miles north of the Gulf, we subtracted ninety-one miles from the stated miles on the map to calculate how many more miles we had to travel to reach our destination.

In the beginning it took us a few days of studying to learn how to interpret the maps and figure out where we were. I have to admit there were times when we didn't know where we were. Some of the problems we had were due to the outdated maps. The second book was printed in 1959, but the navigation miles from Cairo to the Gulf of

24

Mexico were calculated in 1938-1939 and 1940. In a nutshell, we could have canoed fewer or more miles to New Orleans.

As the river became wider, we navigated as much as a half mile from the main channel. But as long as we could see the buoys we knew we were on the main river and not off in a dead-end slough. From this point on, the river is often a mile or more wide, with currents going in all directions, islands, backwaters, and dead-end sloughs. Without the buoys to guide us, we surely would have gotten lost more than once. We oftentimes had to paddle in dangerous water littered with debris. Had one of these submerged trees popped up under us it would have been the end of our canoe trip. It was a chance we had to take. We also took the chance of being run over by a towboat or fast-moving cruiser. We chose to stay out of the way of larger boats and take our chances of being struck by a submerged tree instead. There were some close calls but no accidents.

Four miles north of Prescott, Wisconsin, we approached the first of twenty-seven locks and dams. We had never seen a lock and dam in our lives, and knew absolutely nothing about what we were supposed to do except paddle into the lock. There was a traffic stop-and-go light at the entrance. The light turned green as the lock opened. There were other craft waiting to go in, too. A cabin cruiser, pontoon boats, fishermen, and a towboat. We two greenhorns, with the smallest craft of all, cautiously paddled in, not knowing what to do next or what to expect. There were small square holes in the lock walls with a steel pipe set vertically within the hole. Lou grasped the pipe to hold us steady. The other boats had kept their engines running, so the water within the lock was boiling and churning. The lock doors on the upriver end closed. The next thing we knew, the water level began to recede, Lou had to let go of the pipe. But, lo and behold, a few feet lower another one appeared. The water was being drained out of the lock until it was at about the same level as the water on the downriver side of the lock. Suddenly the water level stabilized. We felt like we were in a deep hole, nothing but cement walls on either side and high above. The lock doors opened and we let all the larger craft go ahead of us. After the last one left the lock, we paddled out into the river.

What a first-time experience! And, we would do it twenty-six more times. In addition to the experience, we would have an opportunity to converse with other river travelers as well, and on occasion be greeted by the lockmaster himself. After leaving a lock, we would be in very swift-moving water for some distance because of the millions of gallons of water released from the lock. The swiftness and distance was determined by the size of the lock, as some were larger than others.

Chapter 12

Stinky's Capers

As we prepared our supper the first night out of the Twin Cities, we gave a dish of dry cat food to Stinky. We thought he'd really appreciate a change of diet, especially since this food was made just for kittens. He took one sniff and walked off a short distance and began to dig a hole in the sand. We could not figure out what he was up to. Why the hole? After the hole was to his liking, he came back to his special cat food supper. He took a piece and went to the hole and dropped it in. We continued to watch him make fifteen or more trips from his dish to the hole. Finally, he had it all stashed away. He then covered the hole with sand. While Stinky was burying his kitten food, Lou and I were sitting around the campfire having our supper. In moments, he came and sat down between us and looked at each of us with a pleading look which seemed to say, "When are you going to give me my supper?" We got the message! He was as much as telling us that kitten food was not his idea of food. We did as we had in the past. We served his supper—*people food!* There was no question about it, Stinky had, among other things, became a very spoiled kitten. We didn't mind. After all he had been through and had so far survived, he deserved being spoiled, and we enjoyed doing it. When we broke camp the next morning, we left the bag of kitten food behind for any other creature that might eat it. That was the beginning and the end of the kitten food experiment.

We entered Lake Pepin through which the Mississippi flows, at Wacouta, Minnesota. The lake is about twenty miles long and in many places two to three miles wide. The main channel was on or near the west side of the lake. Because of a strong, cold northeast wind, we were forced to hug the east shore with little or no current. It turned out to be a tough day of paddling, but we were able to reach Wabasha, Minnesota, five miles south of the lake by evening. The city police allowed us to camp in a city park near the river. Normally no overnight camping was allowed. We appreciated their bending the rules to accommodate three weary travelers. It wasn't long before a number of Wabasha residents appeared to welcome us to their city and especially to see "THAT kitten named Stinky." One nice man offered to take us into town if we needed any groceries or supplies. Lou was elected to go and I stayed at the campsite with Stinky. We never left our campsite unattended, no matter where we were.

The next day we reached Alma, Wisconsin, where we passed through lock #4. This city, in a sense, was a goal. Before we even started the voyage a friend bet us that we wouldn't even get to the Alma lock. BUT WE DID IT!! Goal number one accomplished.

Stinky adjusted well to being confined to the canoe most of the day. Most days, we went ashore at noon for a lunch break and it gave Stinky a chance to stretch his legs and attend to his "kitten duties." Every evening, weather permitting, Stinky had a new homesite. Wherever the tent was pitched, that was home to him and he always stayed close by. When he saw us take the tent down in the morning and break camp, he would go to the river and sit next to the canoe waiting to be put in. He was always the last "item" to be loaded. Never once during the entire trip did we have to call him to the canoe. I think he really liked riding in the canoe.

Late afternoon on the day we left Wabasha, Minnesota, we went ashore at Fountain City, Wisconsin. The city is located very near the river. I went into town to mail some cards, and Lou stayed with the canoe and Stinky. In my absence, unknown to Lou, Stinky decided to climb a willow tree. He had climbed trees before, but none this large or tall. Lou had tried to call him down . . . NO WAY!! So there he was, at least thirty-five feet up in the tree. He was lying on a limb, with his four legs just dangling on either side of the limb. He appeared to be having the time of his life looking down at us, and probably thinking that we should climb up and join him. We called and called him, and even tried to entice him down with food. No go. He hadn't moved one inch from his original position. There is a saying that "Dogs most often come when called, but cats will take a message and get back to you." Stinky was definitely becoming a cat. I knew then that he would never come down on his own. He was just up too high. Cats sometimes get themselves up higher than they really want to be and then are fearful of attempting a retreat to the ground.

We considered contacting the Fountain City Fire Department for help, but decided against it. If they did help us, it could be very expensive. Not that Stinky wasn't worth it, he certainly was, but we decided to keep trying and ask for help only as a last resort. It was now nearly six P.M. and we had to do something and do it soon. I was elected to climb the tree and hopefully get him down and no accidents in the process. I wasn't too enthused about climbing a willow tree, since they are not the safest tree to climb. As I started up, I tested each and every limb before putting any weight on it. It took me a while to get within reach of him. Then I got to thinking that he might panic and go even higher. I talked to him to keep him calm, and reached out and gently scratched him behind his ears and neck and very carefully removed him from his perch.

Now, the problem: How was I to get down with a kitten in one hand and only one hand to go from limb to limb? Stinky solved the problem all by himself. As I held him to my chest, he hung onto my shirt with all four feet and all the claws in them. The last couple of feet to the ground, I just let myself drop. What a relief! He and I both got down in one piece.

There was a big discussion over what to do about Stinky's tree climbing. As he grew bigger, he might be attracted to bigger trees. We didn't want to face a situation in which it might be impossible to get him down from a tree. We finally decided to buy a small dog harness and light nylon rope that very same day. So, back to town again. Lou got a little red harness and a ten-foot piece nylon rope and a snap for one end.

It only took a few days to harness-train him. He probably didn't like it, but he never fought it. One smart kitten!

CHAPTER 13

Summer Celebrants

As WE MOVED ON down the river toward Cairo, Illinois, we never knew what each new day would bring. The weather was a constant factor in our progress or lack of it. If it just rained we continued paddling, but if it included high winds and thunderstorms we headed to the nearest accessible shore to wait it out or set up camp for the day.

In the upper Midwest, summer doesn't always begin on the predicted date. There were times when we wished we'd had an extra blanket or even our sleeping bags instead of cots. In late June we camped at McGregor, Iowa, and slept with our clothes on and were still cold. Further south we would wish for cool days and nights.

The last Saturday of June was a near disaster for us. The river was overrun with pleasure boats of all kinds in addition to the towboats and barges. There were water-skiers, anglers, large cruisers, party boats, and large speedboats. It seemed that nearly every speedboat that saw us had to come closer to get a better look. When we saw one of them heading toward us, we would swing the canoe around so the bow was directed at their wake to keep from getting rolled over. Some would come barreling toward us and as they got parallel with us would shut the engine down. This would create an even bigger wake. We tried waving approaching boats away from us, but to no avail. They were having fun at our expense. We really began to believe that they would have liked to see us get "dumped" and didn't realize the seriousness of their actions. We also began to suspect that alcohol was a factor in their reckless behavior. No people in their right minds would have conducted themselves as they did.

It became one frightening and miserable day for us. Stinky spent most of the time under the tarp, as we were afraid he'd be bounced out of the canoe. At one point we started up our little motor, thinking it would be better to be motor driven rather than paddling. And, we would be able to leave the "arena" at a greater speed. How wrong we were! We were no match for the speedboats, which refused to let us alone and even became more aggressive when they saw us start our

29

motor. We were "sitting ducks." We turned off the motor, pulled it up out of the water, and began paddling again.

By late afternoon we began to look for a suitable campsite. For a very long way every decent sandbar had been occupied by the weekend boaters the entire day, which prevented us from going ashore early to avoid the heavy boat traffic. There were a few places we could have camped, but the nearby campers had a dog or two, so that was out of the question for us. If we had camped, we'd probably be minus our "Commander in Chief" by morning. After searching the riverbank for over a mile, we finally found an isolated sandbar.

That night, after a late supper, we lost no time in going to bed. We were dead-tired after a rough day of paddling and just trying to stay afloat. The next morning we were on the river by five o'clock. We wanted to be out of the area before the speedboaters were up and out.

Weekends on the upper Mississippi, south of the Twin Cities to Muscatine, Iowa, were generally teeming with weekend campers and boaters. But they were never as aggressive and trouble-making as the speedboats we encountered the last weekend of June. In fact, before and after the June incident many campers and boaters had invited us to come ashore to visit, to share their food and drink. The cold or iced drink was always especially enjoyable. Some even gave us ice, which we rarely had for our small metal cooler. On a hot day, being given ice was almost like being given gold. The cooler, for the most part, was used to store food that could be damaged by the humidity, or that would draw ants.

During a rainstorm, we would sometimes collect the rain runoff from the sandbars or mid-flats and store it in the cooler to use for a sponge bath in the evening. The cooler held about four gallons of water, so we called it a "two-gallon sponge bath." Two gallons for each. Stinky never needed to be bathed, being the kitten he was. He would get himself wet wading and swimming in the river, and even lying in a water run-off, and then proceed to groom and clean himself. He did this at least once a day. We also collected rainwater for drinking and cooking, which we stored in a GI water can. Our clothes, towels, etc. were washed in the river. After a few weeks on the river, they looked and smelled pretty "raunchy," to say the least.

When we arrived at Bellevue, Iowa and set up camp, a good number of the residents came down to the river to visit with us. Of course, nearly everyone wanted to hold and pet Stinky. For the entire voyage he never lacked attention.

During the visit with the townspeople the subject of taking a bath came up. "When, and how, do you women take a bath?" We had to admit that we hadn't had a real bath or shower for quite some time. One of the town's residents said we could go to the one and only hotel in town and shower for free! We promptly accepted the offer. We took turns, so that one of us could stay at the campsite with Stinky. What an exhilarating shower! It was the first time in many days that we felt and maybe smelled clean. It did wonders for our spirits.

CHAPTER 14

Skunk Attack

THE DAY BEFORE WE reached Muscatine, Iowa, we had our first encounter with a wild and sometimes dangerous animal. We had camped on rather solid ground, with grass and clover in abundance—never thinking it was just the kind of terrain that would, in the night, be attractive to a little visitor that thrives on the grubs found in this type of soil.

Since it was a nice evening with no rain in the forecast, we left our wooden food box, along with other supplies and equipment, outside of the tent. That was mistake number one! It was a misty, foggy night with little moonlight.

In the middle of the night I awoke to the feeling of having a heavy weight on my chest. It was Stinky! He was just sitting there like a statue, staring at the tent's screen flap. Then I heard a scratching noise. I too looked out the door and saw this object sticking straight up next to the food box. I couldn't figure out what it was. What I first saw was only its tail. Then I saw the rest of the animal. Black and white striped fur—a skunk! Just what we didn't need. They are frequently called "wood's pussy cats."

We didn't want him anywhere near our tent or equipment and supplies. We had to get rid of him. The problem was making sure we didn't scare him. That could be a disaster for us, for he would probably use his major defense—a healthy spraying of his scent! Even if he didn't touch us, our clothing, tent, equipment, and our bodies—and especially our hair—would immediately absorb the odor, the more so, since it was so humid.

I woke Lou, and she suggested I throw some pretzels, which we had in the tent, out and away from the tent. As quietly as I could, I prepared for the skunk attack. Just in my undies, t-shirt, and tennis shoes, with pretzels in hand, I slowly and softly unzipped the screen door. Yes, the skunk was still rummaging around in our equipment.

Then I made our second mistake. I foolishly told Lou to zip the door, as the mosquitoes were as thick as flies. As I stepped out of the tent, I made one soft whistle to get the skunk's attention. As it turned toward me, I threw the pretzels away from the skunk. It went after the pretzels, but then, suddenly turned and came after me! The skunk was so close to me there wasn't time to yell at Lou to unzip the door. There was no place to go except around the tent. As I ran, the skunk had a definite advantage. The tent had eight rope guy-lines, with stakes about four feet away from the tent. Twice I went around the tent, and he was gaining ground and getting closer to me every moment. Going on the third time around, I yelled at Lou, "open the door, I'm coming in, the next time around." She, of course didn't really know what was going on, except that I was being pursued by the skunk. At the end of the third trip around the tent, I dove head-first into the tent. She quickly zipped the door. And not all too soon, for the skunk came right up to the door and tried to claw and chew its way into the tent. I took some insect repellent and sprayed him in the face. Off he went, never to be seen again.

We believe he had rabies, and that is why he chased me, and why he didn't or couldn't spray his scent, and the reason he didn't eat the pretzels. An animal with rabies in its later stages cannot swallow, so he couldn't eat. It was one experience we will never forget. Had either of us been bitten, it would have been the end of our canoe trip FOR SURE!

CHAPTER 15
Cities of Kindness

THE NEXT DAY WE arrived in Muscatine, another city right on the shore of the river. We had hardly pulled in, looking for a place to pitch our tent, when a newspaper reporter showed up. We asked him if it would be O.K. to camp on the grassy area along the river shore next to the boat docks. He said, "No problem." It was a perfect campsite, except that we felt as if we were camping right on "main street."

We were surprised that he knew so much about us without our telling him anything. He told us that many communities along the river were on the lookout for us. That was good news to us, especially for safety reasons. From the first day we left northern Minnesota, we had been on TV, radio, and in various newspapers. As a result we weren't really strangers to many of the people in the cities and towns where we stopped to camp and restock our supplies.

The grassy spot where we camped had sort of a little park-like atmosphere. All of the benches were occupied by some of the elderly men of the city. Apparently it was a meeting place to exchange the news of the day. Everyone we met treated us with utmost kindness. The newspaper reporter invited us to his apartment to take a shower, if we wished. . . . We wished! Two showers in three days wasn't any too many, especially since the weather was becoming much warmer.

In the early evening, an elderly fisherman came ashore, and after a chat with him, he gave us a small walleye pike for Stinky. Later I cleaned it and cut it in small pieces and offered it to Stinky. Just as I guessed, he wouldn't have anything to do with fish! Sometime later the fisherman reappeared and wanted to know how the kitten liked the fish. "Just great," I said. "He ate it all, and looked for more." I didn't have the heart to tell him the truth. The fisherman left with a grin of satisfaction on his face. We knew now, for sure, Stinky was very definitely a "people food" kitten.

The next morning we left Muscatine. Our next city stop would be Fort Madison, Iowa, seventy-five miles downstream. While in Muscatine, we had called the president of the Jaycees in Fort Madison and told him that we would be there in two days. Earlier we had made arrangements for a stop there as guests of the Jaycees. The timing was perfect, we would arrive late on a Sunday afternoon. When we pulled in at one of several docks, a party of about twenty people were there to greet us, including newspaper and TV reporters and a photographer. Arrangements were made to store our canoe and its contents in a safe and secure place. The contents, of course, did not include Stinky. We were taken to a nearby motel where a room had been reserved for all three of us. We were given time to shower and dress in our "out on the town dress-up clothes." At the very bottom of our knapsacks, we each kept one knit shirt and a pair of jeans which were worn only on special occasions.

The evening had been planned for Lou and me. First, we had a tour of the city and its many places of interest. The George and Jean Alton family had us for dinner at their home after the tour. It was a real treat to sit on a chair and eat from real dishes at a table. Far different from sitting on the ground with a mess kit in our laps, and a hungry kitten sitting between us drooling at the mouth and waiting for his dinner. The Altons were wonderful hosts and we enjoyed our visit with them. They even thought of Stinky, and gave us some food to take back to the motel for him.

When we returned to the motel, the first thing we did was look for Stinky. There was no sign of him, nor did he respond when we called him. Suddenly we spotted a small lump in the middle of one of the beds. There he was, sound asleep, between the spread and the blankets. How he got there without even one ruffle in the spread we'll never know. We believed he was scared to death to be alone. Since the day we found him, he had never been left alone in unfamiliar surroundings, and his first instinct was to hide—which he did very well, and without leaving a telltale sign of where he was except for the small lump in the bed.

We slept like logs that night. After sleeping bags and then cots, we felt like two queens to have a nice soft bed and PILLOW, which was a real pleasure. While on the river we used an item of clothing, such as a folded sweatshirt to act as a pillow. At first Stinky didn't sleep very well. Every once in a while I could feel him pounce on my bed. I think he enjoyed jumping from one bed to the other. Finally he gave into his fatigue and fell asleep under one of the beds. During the night, unbeknown to me, I was bitten by a fairly poisonous spider. It had to have been a spider because he bit me more than once. The bites were in a line; three in all. I had a pretty sore, swollen, and red leg for a few days. It seemed that the more I scratched it, the more it itched. It was ironic that after sleeping in a tent, in the woods, and on sandbars, I should be bitten by a spider in a motel. I was glad we were there for only one night, as I was sure that the spider—he or she— would be back for a second meal of me, Lou, or even Stinky.

CHAPTER 16
The Paddle Wheel Boat

AFTER LEAVING FORT MADISON early the next morning, we had gone only about five miles when we encountered very rough water. At this point the river was about two miles wide. We hugged the west shore, which protected us from the westerly winds, even though the main river channel was on the far side of the river. With the use of field glasses we could keep an eye on the buoy markers on the far shore, which assured us we were on the right track. And, we could see the city of Nauvoo, Illinois, on the east shore. This is one of many historical cities on the shores of the Mississippi. As we paddled by, I couldn't help but think of its historical significance. It was here, in February, 1846, that a vanguard of Mormon pioneers, fleeing persecution in Illinois, crossed the ice-covered Mississippi to the Iowa shore. During the first week, 400 teams and 1,350 Mormons crossed the river. According to history, story, or legend, the river had never before or since frozen as thick or hard to allow this much weight and weeklong traffic. In the summer of 1960 the river at that point was about one mile wide. How wide it was in 1846, I don't think anyone knows. It could very well have been considerably wider, since there were no dams, levees, or bank protection works at that time for river control. Also the amount of snow in the north and the rain would have determined the width of the river.

About six miles further downstream we began looking for a place to pull ashore for lunch and a bit of shade. Stinky had also let us know that he needed a sand pile. Across the river, on the east shore, we could see a large paddle wheel boat anchored on shore. Getting out the field glasses for a better look, we saw a sign that read, "COLD BEER . . . LUNCH." To us, it looked like an old retired boat. Since it was a very hot day, the cold beer sign was a real enticement for us to cross the river. There were still quite strong winds from the west, but in spite of that we decided to cross over.

The wind would be at our backs and it would help us along rather than be a hindrance. There were no towboats and barges or large craft to be seen, which was an added incentive to paddle about a mile for that cold beer and a store-bought lunch. We were also in need of fresh drinking and cooking water. We were across the river in no time at all. The canoe was beached where we could keep an eye on it during our absence. Stinky was harnessed and leashed. By now he was in a real hurry to find a sand pile to his liking. After that was all taken care of, we took him with us toward the boat. There was a ramp from the shore to the deck of the boat. Once on deck, we first thought the boat was abandoned, when all of a sudden we could hear the faint sound of some-one singing to the strumming of a guitar. We followed the sound of music and found an elderly gentleman in a small, empty barroom of sorts. He was a heavyset man, with pure white hair and a neatly trimmed beard and mustache to match. It was obvious that he had spent much of his life on the river, as his face was deeply tanned and weathered. He waved us into the room, but continued playing the guitar and singing. We sat down at a small table with Stinky on my lap. After the song was finished, he came to us and welcomed us to his "neck of the river." In a matter of seconds he spotted Stinky. Oh! Oh!, I thought, he's going to throw us overboard, cat and all. Much to my surprise, Stinky was welcome too. It turned out he was very fond of kittens, and he, in the beginning, had more to say to Stinky than either one of us.

We put in our order for a cold beer, a ham sandwich, and a piece of ham for Stinky. Our host appeared to be chief cook and bottle washer, bar tender, and entertainer, all rolled into one. The lunch was excellent as was our extended visit. He wanted to know all about us, the canoe, and most of all about Stinky. He was full of questions about us and we of him. He told us all about the retired paddle wheel boat, which at one time he captained, and about his life on the river. He told us river stories, some of which he sang in ballad form. To say the least, it was a very interesting lunch break, and we enjoyed the visit far too long. We had arrived at high noon and didn't leave until after 2 P.M. By then, the heat and sun were still very intense and we felt it even more after being in the coolness of the boat and having had a few beers. We had intended, earlier in the day, to go as far as Keokuk, Iowa, but decided instead to cross back over to the west shore and camp. Both of us had a headache from the heat and the beer. That day was the first and last we had a beer on a hot day. Since every day was a hot day from then on to New Orleans, there would be no more beer and lunch stops.

By 2 P.M. the wind had died down some so we had no problem going back to the west shore.

CHAPTER 17

Keokuk Lock

THE NEXT MORNING WE awoke to a rainy day. We decided to stay put until the rain let up. To be very honest, we didn't feel too frisky. Stinky was the only frisky member of the crew that morning.

The rain was coming down quite heavily and was mixed with strong, sporadic wind gusts. The possibility of it turning into a severe storm appeared to be good. We didn't want to be caught in a lock during an electrical storm, such as we had experienced in lock #7 just north of La Crosse. Going through the locks in good weather was hazardous enough for our little craft. Lightning, wind, and rain while trapped in a lock was a no-no for us.

The rain and wind continued throughout the morning. We whiled away the time playing cards. Playing cards and playing with Stinky were our only diversions from the daily routine. There was a "stake" for each game of Canasta. The loser would have to do the dishes or wash the clothes. If the loser of the first game won the second game, however, we'd then be even and have to start all over again. I was not a good Canasta player, so I would most often wind up doing the dishes

37

and even the clothes, too, at times. Stinky would sit and watch. Every once in awhile a little white paw would reach out for a card. After this happened a few times we gave him the joker to play with. His span of interest was very short, however, and it wouldn't be long before the little white paw would be back again.

It wasn't until about 2:30 in the afternoon when the clouds began to thin and the heavy rain became a drizzle. We decided to pack up and move on through the Keokuk lock. Since it was only three or four miles, we could be through the lock and be downriver with plenty of time to find a place to camp for the night. By the time we got the tent down and everything packed into the canoe, the drizzle had stopped and the sun was out in full force. With all the humidity from the rain, it turned into a very muggy day.

It was just minutes after 4 P.M. when we arrived at the lock. The red stop light was on, and the north lock gates were closed, which meant the lock was empty of water and traffic from the south would have first dibs in going through the lock—or so we thought. Suddenly we heard someone call to us. Looking up we saw a man who turned out to be the lockmaster. He said he'd been waiting for us for two days. Then he asked us to come up to the lock office, and directed us on how to get there. After securing the canoe on solid ground about fifty yards or so from the lock, we put Stinky in harness and leash and walked to the lock office via solid ground.

The lockmaster introduced himself and his assistant. It wasn't necessary to introduce ourselves—he knew which one of us was Stinky, although he did have to ask which of us was Lou and which was Dorie. After the introductions were complete we were offered a bottle of pop, which we readily accepted. It was better than the beer we'd had the day before.

Then we were told that the Keokuk lock opened only on the hour, twenty-four hours a day. The reason was that it was the largest lock on the entire river, 1,200 feet long with a 38 foot depth, and held 150 million gallons of water. The expense of opening and closing was much greater than the other twenty-six locks on the river. Since it was only 4:15 we would have to wait until five o'clock. We then asked them how they knew where we were on the river, and when they could expect us at Keokuk. "Well," he said, "The Coast Guard has known of your

38

whereabouts off and on since you left St. Paul." The Coast Guard, when passing through the lock a few days before, told the lockmaster that he could expect us any day soon.

Lou and I looked at each other, and gave each other a nod. Yes, we would tell them where and why we were delayed. So, we told them all about stopping at a retired river boat, about its captain, and about the beer. The lockmaster said, "That's par for the course—you're from the beer state, Wisconsin!" We all laughed and we vowed we would never drink any more beer the rest of our journey. Once was enough!

The lockmaster and his assistant voiced some concern for our safety. Thus far we had had no problems, with snakes, man, or animals, except for the skunk. We all three, including Stinky, were good swimmers. In addition, Lou and I both "packed" a small handgun, which fit very nicely in the back pocket of our jean-shorts. They were only .25 cal. auto guns, generally called a "Saturday Night Special." The lock men were somewhat surprised to hear about the guns. We explained that we were avid deer and partridge hunters and were well acquainted with firearms. Just having them gave us a sense of security. We had also agreed under what circumstances we might decide to use them—mainly, a direct or implied threat to ourselves or our property. We figured for someone to just look into a gun barrel or two would be a deterrent. As we explained our viewpoint that day, we didn't know that sometime later our theory would be put to the test.

A few minutes before five, we looked both north and south and no other craft were in sight. We thanked the lock men for their hospitality, and the fun visit, and quickly took off for our canoe. We paddled toward the lock, but didn't approach too close as the lock was now filling with water just for us in our seventeen-foot canoe. After a short time the red lock light turned green and lock gates opened.

We paddled into the cavernous lock. It was the first time we had ever been in a lock all alone. We moved over toward the cement wall and Lou held on to a metal pipe. The water was nearly to the top of the lock wall when the lockmaster appeared to wish us bon voyage. Soon the water level began to drop, and as it did, Lou would grab on to each next lower metal pipe to keep us steady. We reached the bottom of the lock, and as we looked around, all we could see was thirty-eight feet of concrete on both sides of us. Soon the downstream gates opened to let us out. The water was quite fast for a mile or so because of the emptying of the lock.

It was almost unbelievable that we were the only craft going through the biggest lock on the river. The lock had to be filled with 150 million gallons of water and then minutes later, all let out, just for a canoe, two women, and a kitten. We surely weren't like a large barge carrying tons and tons of logs, fertilizer or whatever. Even so, our passage through the lock was FREE. It was one of the most pleasant and interesting lock passages we had had up to then.

Chapter 18

Quincy Boat Club

AFTER LEAVING THE KEOKUK lock, we paddled only five miles, when just south of Warsaw, Illinois, we found a huge sandbar which was completely devoid of any tree, brush, and even grass. We were lucky the sun had burned up most of the humidity so it didn't feel quite so hot.

While in the canoe we were always barefoot. Before ever stepping out of the canoe we nearly always put on our tennis shoes, whether we waded in the river or stepped on land. Being barefoot in either place could be dangerous. Oftentimes walking on land you could be ankle deep in just sand or calf deep in a mixture of wet sand and muck. Not knowing what foreign object might be underfoot—glass, metal, etc.— we played it safe. With rare exceptions, we always wore our "tennies."

Another reason we wore our tennis shoes on shore was because the sand was usually so hot it burnt your feet, especially in mid or late afternoon. As the saying goes, "It was so hot you could fry an egg on the pavement." If one could fry an egg on sand, in the south we could have had sand-fried eggs every day. The hot sand didn't seem to bother Stinky too much, though. Whenever we went ashore, Stinky was the first item to be unloaded. On an extremely hot day, we'd deposit him in belly-deep water. Most of the time he would just stand there and cool himself off, and after a bit of that, bounce off to investigate his new home for the night.

This day we unloaded the canoe and set up camp about thirty yards from the riverbank. We were able to find enough dry driftwood to build a halfway decent fire for cooking supper. We had just finished supper and I (again) was doing the dishes, when a large fishing boat approached. Ever the cautious two, we went to the shore and more or less interviewed our visitor. Whenever any boat approached our campsite, we always tried to be on the riverbank before they had time to land and enter our campsite. After some minutes of talking back and forth, he told us he was an officer with the Keokuk Police Department, and had we stayed in Keokuk for the night, he had a cabin there we could have used. We felt he could be trusted, so we invited him to our campsite. Now, one must remember: This was 1960 when, for the most part, people could be trusted—and this man was trustworthy. Today, I would hesitate to invite a complete stranger into my campsite, regardless of what he says or how he looks.

This police officer had lived on the river all of his life and was an avid fisherman. He had a lot of safety tips for us, particularly about snakes. There was one tip we hadn't heard before. He warned us not to paddle too close to shore, since snakes were known to drop out of the trees and into boats. If this was true or not, we never found out. Maybe they do back in the sloughs, but on the main river I don't remember seeing any trees hanging over the riverbank. At least not in the south. Maybe he was just pulling our leg.

We had been wary of snakes for some time, especially in the early morning when we packed to leave a campsite. We took care when turning the canoe over, taking down the tent (which had a floor), and moving other camp equipment that had been left outside overnight. Never, during the entire 2,300+ miles, did we ever see a snake. Not even a common garter snake. On occasion, we did see belly tracks of snakes in the sand.

After a nice visit with the Keokuk police officer, he left, saying, "See you again soon." We said, "OK," at the same time not believing we really would. The next day we got up before the sun to try and get in a few miles before it really got hot. We passed through lock #20 south of Meyer, Illinois. Now the state of Missouri was on the west side of the river. We continued on to Quincy, a total of twenty-nine miles for a day's paddling.

41

It was late afternoon when we arrived in Quincy. Since it was close to the river and a good-size city, we didn't expect to find a place to camp for the night. Then we saw a sign: Quincy Boat Club. We pulled in and Lou went to the club's door, but it was locked. She began knocking on the door because she could hear voices inside. As she suspected, it was a "key club"—members only! As she started to return to the canoe, the door opened. And there he was! None other than the police officer from Keokuk, Iowa.

For a minute we thought our eyes were playing tricks on us. He greeted us warmly and invited us in, Stinky included. He didn't have his boat this time. He had arrived at the club by car. After talking with him and others in the club, the conversation finally turned to where we could find a camping site for the night. It was getting late in the day and it was beginning to rain. The bartender told us there was some space off to the side of the club and we could camp there if we wanted to. We readily accepted the offer. We left Stinky in the care of the police officer and got busy unloading the canoe as the rain was increasing in volume and intensity.

After we got the tent up and everything stashed away, we went back into the club to retrieve Stinky. We were then told that there was a faucet under the club where we could take a shower. We accepted that offer, too. Yes, there was a faucet with a showerhead. But what they didn't tell us was that it had only cold water. *Icy* cold water! We were already soaking wet from the rain, which was much warmer than the faucet water. Shower we did, cold water or not, and changed into dry clothes, utilizing our ponchos.

The second stint of cleaning up came when we were offered the use of the women's restroom to wash our hair with WARM water. Stinky, during all of this, sat on the policeman's lap. Now I could see he was getting restless. It was time for him to be given the opportunity to do his thing. I tucked him into my poncho and took him under the building where it was dry and sandy. Stinky wasted no time and when he was finished, I put him in the tent, as he was due for a "cat nap." When I returned to the club, I found that the policeman had offered his car to us so we could go to a grocery store for supplies. He would keep an eye on our canoe, tent, etc. Off we went shopping. We couldn't believe our good fortune again. Ninety-nine percent of the people we met on the river were not only good to us, but were of great help in many, many ways. Thanks to them, we accomplished our goal.

CHAPTER 19

A Long, Hard Day

THE EVENING BEFORE WE left Quincy, we were told by the people at the Club that there was a nice camping spot across the river from Louisiana, Missouri, on the Illinois side. It was ONLY about forty-four miles downriver from Quincy. I use the term "only" loosely.

The next morning we got up at four o'clock and were on our way by five. The rain had stopped and it looked as if we were to have a nice day—without rain. The camping spot was to be our goal for the day. We passed through lock #21 just south of Quincy without incident. By noon we had gone about eighteen miles and were in Mark Twain waters, none other than Hannibal, Missouri. Because we were pinched for time, we didn't stop. We did take special interest in the highway bridge spanning the river which was named for Mark Twain.

Eight miles south of Hannibal, we passed through lock #22, again without incident. As we approached Gilberts Island, we chose to leave the main channel on the Illinois side of the river and continue on the Missouri side. We saved ourselves about two miles of paddling, because the channel cut back to the Missouri side south of the large island.

So far things were going well, and it appeared we would reach our goal for the day. We took only one short break, at noon, mostly to let Stinky do his thing and stretch his limbs. We ate lunch while paddling. Now we would be passing small towns, but all we could see of them were the rooftops of the buildings because of levees and embankments that protected them from early spring flooding. About three in the afternoon, we calculated that, according to the river map, we still had ten miles of paddling to reach our designated campsite. Our canoe speed was 3.5 miles per hour, which meant we would arrive about six. It would be a long, hard day, nearly thirteen hours of paddling.

When we began our journey, we mistakenly thought we could just let the current carry us downriver, and sit back and enjoy the ride. With a river current of approximately seven miles an hour (summer 1960) we figured we could easily cover about fifty miles a day without working too hard. *How wrong we were!* We failed to take into account weather, winds, erratic currents, sandbars, large boats, barges, going through the locks, AND losing our way from time to time. So far we had been covering about thirty-five miles per day. Some days more, and some days no miles at all. The weather—storms, tornadoes, cold in the north and extreme heat in the south—were our constant adversaries. The weather was in total control of our progress, or lack of it, every day, the entire journey.

As we neared the much talked about campsite, we crossed over to the Illinois side of the river. The river was only about one-half mile wide at this point. Soon we spotted a pontoon boat anchored near shore. This must be the campsite we were aiming for all day. A man, a woman, and two children were on shore. We wondered if we would be intruding on their privacy. No problem, for when they saw us approach they yelled a welcome and waved us in to join them. How lucky could we get?

It wasn't necessary for us to tell them who we were. They knew! Our names, Lou and Dorie, were painted on both sides of the bow and stern of the bright red and white canoe, as well as our origination and destination. We also looked the part. It was obvious we weren't out for a casual afternoon of paddling. The canoe was heavily loaded, we were deeply tanned (almost to a crisp), and of course the presence of Stinky lying on the bow made for positive identification.

Stinky became an instant playmate for the children and they for him. He just wallowed in all the attention they gave him. We didn't worry about his biting or scratching them, even though he had all of his claws on all four feet. He never displayed any aggressiveness during play with humans. In a short time the same old question arose: "We heard you wanted to find a home for him. Will you give him to us?" We told them it was many weeks ago that we had thought of finding him a home. But we now have become so attached to him, and he has become too much a part of our adventure. We would miss him and he would miss us. He was enjoying his very unusual and enchanting

44

"kittenhood." When we told them of some of his adventures and mishaps, they agreed that his life would be somewhat drab, living with them, in comparison to his life of high adventure on the river.

Unfortunately, after thirty-nine years, I do not remember the family's name, but I do remember their kindness to us. The parents and children helped us unload our canoe and even offered to help pitch our tent. The campsite was the best we'd had in some time. A nice sand beach—NO MUD! There were patches of grass here and there away from the shore where we could pitch our tent. There was a cooking grill, benches, and of all things—a *table!* Nothing could be nicer. Since they were using the grill, we began to gather wood to build a fire to cook our supper. They told us not to bother as they were going to have us join them for supper—a meal of catfish with all the trimmings, including a cold drink with ICE! It was something we hadn't seen or tasted in a while. Ice was something we rarely had. When we did, it was always given to us by friendly campers or fishermen. We would store it in our little metal cooler. It never lasted more than eight or ten hours and then we'd have drinking water. Nothing was ever wasted, not even water. This campsite was the very last "prepared" campsite we would have for the balance of our journey, which was then more than a thousand miles to New Orleans.

Our newly found, temporary friends left us shortly before dark. It wasn't long before we hit the sack. It had been a long day of paddling but it was well worth it. Stinky fell asleep within minutes—all played out for a change.

CHAPTER 20

Lock #25 Hospitality

THE NEXT MORNING WE were up early and on the river by five o'clock. When we first began our journey in Northern Minnesota we didn't get up until six, which is the coldest time of day. Now, as we were entering a warmer climate, we shed ourselves of sleep anywhere between 3 and 4 A.M. We didn't have or need an alarm clock—Stinky took it upon himself to be a very dependable clock—which didn't need winding up. Either Lou or I would suddenly feel a soft little paw pat our face and then he'd proceed to pick in our hair to make sure we would wake up and get going. It was his way of saying, "Time to get up." It is known that all animals and birds have clocks and even calendars in their heads. They know when to wake up, go to sleep, migrate, and hibernate. Truly amazing! Stinky was a shining example of when to wake up and when to go to sleep.

Being on the river by four or five in the morning was one way to beat the heat and have at least a few hours of comfortable paddling. From 10 A.M. to 4 in the afternoon was the hottest time of day. Looking for a place to camp for the night usually began at four, and most often we were successful within an hour or two.

Ten miles south of the sumptuous campsite we passed through Lock #24. Only two more to go. Lock #27 is on the Chain Of Rocks Canal which we did not have to pass through. After paddling thirty miles we decided to call it a day, and made camp on an island a few miles north of Cap Au Gris, Missouri, and Lock #25.

After paddling well over a thousand miles, the Great River was beginning to have its effects on both Lou and me, maybe even Stinky. Even though we always camped well away from the shore, I would, in my sleep, hear the river and its lapping the shore even if it wasn't. I would experience a real feeling of my cot bobbing up and down like the canoe did during the day. It was a weird sensation that would continue for the rest of the trip and even for a few weeks after it was finished. On the trip, I actually got up in the night a couple of times to check the river, thinking it had risen during the night. The noise of the river seemed to be right at the door of our tent. There were times when the river did rise during the night, but we were never in any danger of being flooded out.

The next day, after only a few hours on the river, we arrived at Lock #25. The lockmaster was waiting for us. He was concerned! Information given to him as to our whereabouts should have had us at Lock #25 two days earlier. Again we knew, people were keeping an eye on us.

He said, "If you women aren't too busy, my family and I would like you to attend a picnic with us and then spend the evening at our home." Lockmasters' homes are always located very near the lock. After a phone call or two he was able to find us help in getting the canoe and all our gear up near the lock office where it would be secure for the rest of the day and that night.

He then called his wife, and she came down to the lock to meet us and take us up to their house. Now our biggest concern was Stinky. He was harnessed and leashed, but would he be welcome in their home? If not, we wondered what we would do with him, since we couldn't "store" him in the tent. Our fears were soon put aside as he was more than welcome. They didn't have a cat or dog, so Stinky wouldn't be a problem.

As we entered the home, we were steered to the bedroom we would have for the night, and our own private bath. We were then told we could do any washing of clothes we might have. We couldn't understand—why all of this for us? She said they were waiting for us to arrive and had planned in advance that we were to be their guests. Lou went back to the canoe and collected all the clothes, towels, etc. that needed a good washing, which meant very nearly everything we owned. The white and dark were not separated for washing. By now all that was once white had become a dirty gray color from river washing and all of it smelled of the river.

We took our much needed baths and added the clothes we had worn to the mounting pile of wash. For the second time we donned our special occasion clothes for the picnic. The baths got the river smell off of us and for the first time in a while I felt and smelled clean. I have to admit that after the bath I couldn't believe how dirty the water was, nor the grubby ring around the tub. By this time I had a deep tan. Some of it, much to my chagrin, was plain baked-on, ground-in dirt! I always believed there were two kinds of dirt, clean and dirty. I salved my pride by deciding that I was dirty from clean dirt. That made me feel better.

Initially we weren't too enthused about going to a picnic. Thus far, it seemed like most of our meals were somewhat like a picnic—eating outside. This picnic proved to be quite different from our so-called picnics, however. For one thing, the food was scrumptious in comparison to our bland, Spartan meals. The people we met (friends of the lockmaster and his wife) treated us as if we were royalty, and

Stinky a very royal kitten. We again found many people who were following our progress via radio, TV, and newspapers. Lock #25 was one of the best rest stops we had encountered: clothes laundered, a luxurious bath, a fun picnic, and sleeping in a bed.

The next morning Stinky woke us up at five o'clock. Luckily it didn't disrupt our hosts. They served a great breakfast of bacon, eggs, toast, and coffee made with real tap water. It was the kind of breakfast we hadn't had in a long time. Our hosts helped us put the canoe in the river and load it. By six o'clock we were on our way. Our rest stop wasn't soon to be forgotten.

Chapter 21

The Big Muddy

As we traveled on south, the Great River was beginning to change its behavior. The main channel was always there with its buoy markers, sometimes marked with lights. There were many more large and small islands which caused the river to separate from the channel. This slowed the current in the main channel and made for erratic currents. There was no sitting back and just letting the canoe drift as we had done on occasion on the upper Mississippi. We wondered, "Is this the way it's going to be all the way to New Orleans?"

Just north of Grafton, Illinois, the Illinois River entered the Mississippi. We hardly noticed it because it didn't increase the current as we had expected it might. By late afternoon we arrived at Alton, Illinois, and passed through Lock #26 . . . the very LAST lock, and under a huge railroad and highway bridge. A half-mile further downstream we found a nice, small plot of sand on the Missouri side of the river and set up camp for the night. We barely got ourselves settled when a group of fishermen and women arrived and anchored just off shore from our campsite. Clearly it must have been a good fishing hole. Most of them stayed well past dark, which eliminated any chance of bathing for us. We were glad we'd had a nice bath in a tub the day before. Even so, we felt "sticky dirty" from being in the hot sun all day.

We played with Stinky every evening, so he'd use up some of his pent-up energy and, more important, to give him some exercise after being in the canoe all day. Lou and I didn't have to worry about getting exercise. We got all we needed. We hit the sack and all three of us slept like the dead. It had been a long, hot, skin-blistering day. But the days to come would be even hotter!

The next morning we had gone only six miles and we noticed a distinct change in the color of the river water. It had become a muddy-red. Looking behind us, we could see the Missouri River flowing into the Mississippi. Again, no significant change in the current was noticeable, only the change in color. The color change would be with us for a mile or two, until it faded away in the greater waters of the Mississippi.

We had been looking forward to seeing the Missouri River, but we were somewhat disappointed because it was much smaller than we had expected. There was a sand and mud bar of considerable size on the west shore of the Missouri where it entered the Mississippi. When the river is "running high" this bar would be under water, and the mouth of the Missouri would be about one mile wide. Because the water was low in 1960, however, it was only about one-half mile wide.

Now that we were though all the locks and dams in the upper and middle Mississippi, which control the river and make river traffic possible, there were many, many more levees, embankments, and bank protectors. This was especially true where cities and towns were located near the river. Every bend in the river had bank protection. Now the river would truly live up to its reputation as it meandered to New Orleans and the Gulf of Mexico. It followed a path of least resistance, as it had for thousands of years.

CHAPTER 22

St. Louis, Missouri

As WE TRAVELED ON south, the river map indicated that the river was getting narrower. We found this to be true, especially above and below St. Louis. In some places it was no more than a quarter-mile wide and oftentimes even less. This was due to the extremely large sand and mud bars that extended off the shore and into the river. The sand and muck islands caused the river to split around them. More than once we found ourselves in a dead-end slough.

As the river became narrower, we cranked up the little motor. With river traffic at a peak, we needed more power than two paddles could provide. Stinky was removed from the bow, his favorite sightseeing perch, and parked in the middle of the canoe on the top of the canvas tarp. It was a relatively safe place for him. He could still watch all that was going on around us. That was right up his alley! Sightseeing, digging holes, wading, and chasing bugs were his main interests.

We were frequently in the midst of tows (towboats are often called simply "tows") pushing large numbers of barges, sometimes as many as thirty or forty, lined up four barges across. This made for even less room for us to stay clear of them. In addition to the barges and tows we had the company of large cabin cruisers, fishing boats, speedboats, and—least expected—water skiers! I thought I must be dreaming. I couldn't imagine why anyone would even consider skiing in the polluted waters of the Mississippi while being surrounded by heavy river traffic. We didn't only look small, we *felt* small amid the heavy river traffic, massive in both size and numbers. Another pair of eyes in the back of our heads would have been of immense help.

St. Louis, the chief city of Missouri, was established in 1736. In the late 1700s it became a fur trading post for both European and Native American trappers. It continued to be so for more than a hundred years. St. Louis also became the crossroads for Westward Expansion. It was the starting point for exploring parties, including that of Louis and Clark. Many parties of wagon trains rendezvoused at St. Louis to prepare for the trek across the plains. Others gathered to pole rafts up the Missouri, sometimes as far as the river's head-waters in northern Montana.

For many years there has been a controversy concerning the Mississippi and Missouri rivers: Is the Missouri a tributary of the Mississippi or is the Mississippi a tributary of the Missouri? As far as I know, It's been decided that the Missouri is a tributary of the Mississippi.

The cities of St. Louis, Missouri, and East St. Louis, Illinois, bound both shores of the river for twenty miles. We had to deal with the "God Awful" traffic and bedlam the entire twenty miles. Passing through these two cities via the river was an experience never to be wanted again. We didn't know it then, but there would be more of the same as we neared New Orleans.

As we moved downriver on the Missouri side, both sides of the river were heavily industrial. Steel companies, oil companies, chemical companies, wharfs, and docks and more docks! Barges loading and unloading made it one big, busy place! It didn't look as if there would be any place for us to pull ashore without getting run over.

Finally we saw a sign: Mound City Boat Club. It was just what we were looking for. We motored into one of the empty boat slips and in minutes a very nice man came to welcome us to St. Louis. It wasn't long before two newspaper reporters as well as a TV crew showed up. Yes! Like celebrities we did feel. I think Stinky did too, as he always enjoyed meeting people. As soon as someone new held him, his little "purr motor" would kick in. Real contentment! After the interviews and filming were completed, we restocked our fresh water, gas for the motor, and kerosene for the lantern. The man who greeted us at the dock warned us that a storm was brewing and there wouldn't be a place to camp for the next several miles, as we would still be in the city. We started up the motor, since the river traffic was still very heavy and would be for some time. We had to make those several miles as soon as possible. I told the little motor, "Please, don't conk out now, we need you."

We hadn't gone but a few miles when we encountered mighty rough water. Along with the heavy river traffic it was no picnic. Stinky was put UNDER the tarp. Even with the help of the motor we struggled with the storm. Heavy winds, high hazardous waves, and buckets of rain required us to sponge out the canoe every few minutes. The heavily loaded canoe had only about five or six inches of freeboard. We had not only the rain to deal with, but also water splashing in the canoe from the waves. The storm lasted for more than an hour and then the rain turned into a constant drizzle. We shut off the motor and began sopping the water that had accumulated in the canoe. But we were out of the city of St. Louis, now, and we could begin to look for a place to camp for the night. All three of us were storm-beaten and ready to call it quits for the day. It was late afternoon before we found a suitable campsite.

Before the canoe was unloaded completely, we pitched the tent and threw Stinky in where he could dry himself and stay dry. This evening we would have to cook our supper in the tent on the tiny gas stove. All the driftwood around us, which normally we would have used for a fire, was saturated with rain.

By the time we finished supper the rain had stopped. After getting everything squared away outside of the tent and the canoe pulled up well away from shore, we discovered that Stinky was nowhere to be seen. Never before had he strayed from a campsite. We began a frantic search. He had always been very responsive when he was called, but not this time! I really began to worry that he had gotten into serious trouble. Lou went upriver along the shore and I went downriver. Not too far from our camp I heard a mournful meowing. There he was, in exactly the same kind of mess he was in when we first found him. He was in a small slough, stuck in muck up to his belly. The rain had softened the muck and he broke through while attempting to walk across it. By the time I reached him, I was up to my knees in the black, gooey, putrid muck. I had to pull his legs out one at a time. Stinky was truly a stinky kitten again.

I yelled to Lou that I had found him. After I cleaned the muck off him and myself, we headed for the tent, for what I hoped would be a good night's sleep. It had been one awesome, lousy day for the most part, and I was glad it was over. Tomorrow, another day.

CHAPTER 23

Guns Come Out

AFTER BEING ON ROUGH and choppy water all day, sleep was hard to come by. I'd doze off, but it felt as if my cot were moving up, down, and sideways, just as the canoe had done all day. In all truth, I never did sleep well the entire time on the river.

Suddenly I was jerked wide-awake by the sound of metal striking metal. I lay for a few moments trying to imagine what could be causing the sounds I thought I'd heard. Then I heard it again. No, it wasn't a dream or figment of my imagination, it was real! Trying to be as quiet as I could, I crept toward the screen flap. Since it wasn't a very dark night, I could see a shadowy figure trying to remove the motor from its mount on the canoe. Using my foot, I gave Lou a nudge. She also had heard the noise, and was wide awake. We knew we couldn't talk, not even whisper. All communication was by hand signals. We got our guns and two flashlights out of our knapsacks. With a gun in one hand and a flashlight in the other, we stepped out of the tent and quietly approached the figure, who was facing away from us. We were able to come within about ten yards when we turned on our flashlights and confronted the person with a loud HEY!! When the figure spun around, we saw that it was a young boy, no more than fifteen or sixteen years old. We kept our lights directly in his face and our guns in plain view. He had the most startled look on his face, the kind I'd never seen before or since on anyone. He was told in no uncertain terms to "git" and don't come back or he'd be shot where it would hurt most. "Git" he did! One fast run to the river and he rowed away as fast as he could.

Granted, we maybe were a little rough on the boy, especially verbally, but we couldn't afford to take any chances. Long before, we came to an agreement as to when and how we would use our guns if necessary. Under no circumstances would we be wimps. Anything we said or did would be aggressive and to the point. Any person or persons who might give us a hard time would soon find we meant business. Our "pact for survival" paid off more than once.

The rest of the night, we took turns sleeping and guarding ourselves and our property. The shock of the first and unexpected confrontation stirred my mind. What if there would have been two or more thieves, not only one? And what if they were older? Then, what would we have done? This was something we would have to talk about. Some might not be thieves, instead just mischief makers. We had to make plans for possible future confrontations, and they had to be well-laid plans.

For quite some time before that night, we hadn't had the guns on our person; they were just tucked away in our knapsacks. That night told us we weren't as safe as we thought. From then on we kept our guns in their holsters on a belt or in our jeans back pocket whenever on shore for whatever reason. At night, the guns were in our cots with us. That night taught us and our intruder an inexpensive lesson, and no one got hurt. The boy knew we meant what we said.

The following morning we finally got a few uninterrupted hours of sleep. We both slept well past our usual four o'clock wake-up time.

CHAPTER 24

Grounded

THE NEXT TWO DAYS went by without incident. The second day we camped on a large sandbar across the river from Crystal City, Missouri. About a hundred yards downriver, on the same sandbar, two large pontoon boats were anchored. A dozen or more people were having a picnic on the shore. It wasn't long before three young women came to our campsite. They said they didn't know who we were or what we were doing on the Mississippi until they spotted Stinky, and that "rang a bell." They knew then that we must be the two women paddling the Mississippi to New Orleans.

They invited us to come to their picnic, meet their friends, and have a drink with them, an invitation which we readily accepted. In the end it was more than just a drink. They insisted on giving us food and ice. When we returned to our campsite we were loaded down with eggs, bread, canned goods, and the first butter we had had in weeks. There was enough ice to nearly fill our cooler. The ice would last only a day or two, so everything we ate for the next two days had butter on it, since the butter would melt and turn rancid without ice. We boiled half the eggs, because then we'd still have eggs even though the ice was gone. Even Stinky got his share of eggs and butter—a new food experience for him.

When we broke camp the next morning, the pontoons were still anchored, everyone on board sound asleep. At 10 A.M., after several hours paddling, we took a shore break. It was going to be one hot day. After a half-hour break in the shade, we hit the water again. Every day since leaving St. Paul, Minn. we had been taking salt tablets to replace salt lost through physical exertion and the heat.

We soon found another use for the sponges, other than soaking up water in the canoe on a rainy day. Soaking the sponges in the river and squeezing them out on our heads had a cooling effect; never mind the smell of the water or some of the assorted items we would see floating on the surface. We had passed small towns and cities near or on the river's shore where raw sewerage was piped directly into the river. You name it, we saw it floating in the river. There were times when it was not wise to cool off with river water.

I think Lou could take the heat better than I could. There were many days when I hated to see the sun come up. On some mornings there would be a few clouds, and I'd think, "Maybe it will be partly cloudy today." But by mid-morning the heat of the sun would burn the clouds away. We had either full sun or heavy clouds with rainstorms. It seemed there was nothing in between, like "partly cloudy and cool."

By late afternoon we had made about thirty-five miles and decided to start looking for a place to camp for the night. Paddling close to shore, just north of Claryville, Missouri, the canoe came to a sudden halt. We were grounded on something, and we didn't know what. We couldn't move the canoe over the obstruction and we couldn't back off because of the very strong current. The current was stronger because the river channel was very narrow due to a long and broad sandbar on the east shore.

There we sat, unable to go forward or backward. The river was too deep and swift to allow us to lighten the canoe by getting out and pushing it over the obstacle. Even if we could, we'd have a heck of a time getting back in the canoe and bringing it under control. After weighing the pros and cons, we decided it was best to try to go forward by shifting the weight in the bow toward the stern end of the canoe. We moved everything from the forward end of the canoe, except Lou, to the back. It wasn't long before the canoe moved enough so that the middle of the canoe was firmly stuck. We then moved everything to the bow end, including items that were originally in the back.

The strategy worked, and as the canoe slid over the obstruction, my paddle struck a hard, solid object. Later, in looking at the river map, we found that we had struck submerged "contraction works." Contraction works, levees, revetments, and embankments for protection of the river's bank line the shore from St. Paul to New Orleans. Never before had we been in this type of risky situation. We got into the trouble because we paddled too close to the shore—a lesson not to be forgotten.

Two miles south of Claryville, Missouri, we found a nice sandbar with plenty of driftwood for a cooking fire. As Lou stepped out of the canoe onto the sand, she discovered it was too hot to stand on barefoot. That afternoon and very nearly every day thereafter, we put on our tennis shoes before stepping on shore. The sand was just too hot for bare feet. Stinky found his own solution in dealing with hot sand. As soon as he was put on shore, he would walk into the river and just stand belly deep in water. After a bit of that, he would lie on the river's edge with his feet in the water. One smart kitten.

After unloading the canoe and pulling it up on shore, the next task was pitching the tent. After it was up it would give us a small amount of shade. It was an easy tent to erect: one tee-bar, eight base stakes, and eight guy lines. It was seven by seven, and seven feet high. Very comfortable for two people and a kitten. After many days of putting it up, we could now perform the task in ten minutes or so.

In the South there were rarely any trees or brush of any kind on the sandbars close to the river's edge. The only place to offer trees or brush near the shore was swamp and muck, not suitable for camping. After we had pitched the tent, one of us would go to the nearest tree or brush line, chop down ten or fifteen small bush-like trees six to ten feet tall, tie them together with a rope, and drag them back to the camp. How much we cut depended on how far they had to be dragged and how hot it was.

How much we cut also determined what we would build for shade. Sometimes we simply stuck the trunks deep into the sand, which made them look like growing trees, or we would build a lean-to, which would take more time and more trees. There were times when we would have to walk a city block or more to acquire the brush and trees we needed for shade. Even so, we did it every day except when it rained. After being on the river most of the day without a bit of shade, the shade we made for ourselves was a tremendous relief from the glare and heat of the sun.

That night near Claryville was almost sleepless. We had camped directly across river from the Southern Illinois Sand Company. Whatever they were doing over there, they did it all night long. It was so noisy, it sounded as if they were on our side of the river. That evening was the last time we camped anywhere near a sand company.

CHAPTER 25

On to Cairo

WHEN LOOKING AT THE river map the next morning, we saw that we still had a little over a hundred miles to go to reach Cairo, Illinois. And another 875 miles to New Orleans. Baring anything unforeseen, we should reach Cairo in two and a half days. Our food and water supplies were beginning to dwindle. The water we had gotten in St. Louis was now nearly gone, so we decided to ration what little we had left. It would be for drinking only. For cooking we would have to use purified river water. Our food supply had been increased by the picnickers, but we'd added nothing since then. Many food staples were either low or depleted. We passed small towns near the river, but none with easy access because of levees or revetments. All we could see were the rooftops of buildings.

After paddling nearly forty miles, we made camp on Hanging Dog Island, on the Illinois side of the river. We had a good supply of pancake mix, and we had some dried fruit which we cut into small pieces and added to the batter. The fruit replaced the jam, jelly, or syrup which we no longer had. It was a meager supper but filling. That evening, we made a long grocery list for the first opportunity we would have to go shopping.

For breakfast the next morning we had pancakes again. For lunch, it was cold pancakes left over from breakfast. I think Stinky maybe wondered why it was always pancakes. When he found there wasn't anything else he would, after a little coaxing, eat his share. And, yes, we had pancakes for supper, too!

When we ran out of oleomargarine, we would substitute colored vegetable shortening. We used the shortening mainly for frying, rather than liquid oil, which came in glass bottles then, rather than plastic as it does today. The fewer of those heavy glass bottles, the better. Adding a little salt to the shortening made it look like oleomargarine, and it moistened pancakes and biscuits like oleo. But it sure didn't fool our taste buds.

Our chance to shop came sooner than we expected. The next day, as we neared Cape Girardeau, Missouri, we decided to start the motor, since the river channel was quite narrow and the river traffic heavy. But despite all the pulling of the starter rope, it just refused to start. Threading our way through traffic, we arrived at the northern outskirts of the city. The river map indicated that Cape Girardeau had a city wharf. It was just what was needed. A short distance downriver we found the wharf among all sorts of piers and docks, and soon we found a spot to tie up the canoe.

The first order of business was to find someone who could fix the motor. We had to have it in running condition in case of an emergency. Second, grocery shopping was a must! After asking a number of people on the wharf, we found that there was an engine repair shop and a small grocery store, both nearby. Luck was with us—motor repair and grocery shopping all in just one stop. Lou stayed with Stinky and the canoe while I left with the motor to find the repair shop. A couple of blocks from the wharf I found the shop. I was told that the motor probably needed a new plug and a carburetor cleaning, since it had been exposed to a lot of rain and wind-blown sand.

Since the repairman wasn't very busy, he would have it ready in about an hour. He could tell from my accent that I wasn't from his "neck of the woods." As I began to tell him where my partner was,

Above: Dorie and Lou take a breather in Muscatine, Iowa. **Below left:** Lou holds a cleaned-up Stinky, found early in the trip near Grand Rapids, Minnesota. **Below right:** Stinky quickly adapted to canoe, tent and life on the Mississippi.

Above: Bovine curiosity at Jacobsen, Minnesota. **Below:** Stinky waits patiently for Lou to put him into the canoe for another day of paddling.

Above: A typical campsite in the hot and humid south. The brush on the right is a lean-to, quickly built by Dorie and Lou for shade. **Below left:** The "Commander in Chief" claims his favorite spot on the bow of the canoe. **Below right:** What appeared to be a clean sandbar turned into thick, black muck after a heavy rain.

New Orleans!

After two months, more than 2,300 miles of winding river, lightning storms, tornados, blazing sun, unrelenting heat and humidity, muck and mire, river traffic, mosquito and black fly hordes, unsavory river characters, and tedium, Dorie and Lou, with Stinky, make a triumphal entrance into New Orleans. Here they are being greeted on the wharf by two representatives of the Sheraton Charles Hotel, where the three were guests of honor.

and where we were heading, he suddenly stopped me and asked if we still had the kitten with us. I didn't have to say any more. He knew from TV and newspapers all about us. The grocery store was about six blocks away, and he offered me the use of his car to get our much-needed supplies. I spent about an hour shopping in the air-conditioned store. It felt so good I hated to leave and go back into the heat.

The temperature in the store was about sixty-five degrees with no humidity. Outside, the heat and humidity were stifling. It was like going out of a deep freeze into an oven. I bought quite a lot, since we were out of so many things and very low on others. It was a good thing I had a car to haul them back to the wharf. There were three large grocery bags full of food—lots of canned goods, dried fruit, powdered milk, jams and jellies, canned stew meat, bacon, Spam, and even a few fresh potatoes. To top it off, one dozen fresh eggs. We would boil most of the eggs to preserve them for a number of days. With the new groceries, we wouldn't have to stop for food buying for at least two weeks. We would count on rainstorms to replenish our water when necessary.

It was well past noon before all of the errands were finished, including the filling of every empty container we had with precious, fresh, clean water. We put the motor on the mount and on the very first pull of the starter rope, it RAN! The new spark plug and carburetor cleaning did the trick. Just as were ready to leave, a newspaper reporter appeared. After pictures and an interview, we left Cape Girardeau by motor until we were out of the heavy river traffic.

Since we had spent a better part of the day in Cape Girardeau, we continued paddling downriver until early evening. Finally we found a tremendous sandbar, across the river from Willard, Illinois, for a campsite that night. We celebrated by making an unusually special supper—salmon patties, baked potatoes, creamed peas, and rolls. It took a while to put it all together, and as a result we ate in the dark with only a small fire and the kerosene lantern for light. All three of us enjoyed the supper—especially after four consecutive pancake meals.

The next morning we were up early and on the river by 5:30 A.M. Our goal for the day was Cairo, Illinois, which was about twenty-seven miles downriver. Since we had stocked up on everything we needed at Cape Girardeau, there was no need to go ashore at Cairo.

Just eight miles short of reaching Cairo, an sudden rainstorm hit us. Up until then the heat and humidity had been almost insufferable. We were dressed with the least possible amount of clothing. The rain came in a steady downpour. We sopped up the water with sponges as fast as we could. Having added more weight (the maximum the canoe could hold) with groceries and containers of water, we didn't need, nor could we afford, any more weight from the rain. As it was, we had only about four or five inches of freeboard.

The rain continued to pelt us for more than two hours. It was, what we would soon learn, a "rain squall." They appear suddenly and disappear quickly. But this one was the longest squall we ever encountered. All we did was sponge water, paddle a few strokes, and sponge some more. After the ferocious heat, the first half hour of rain felt good. But then we began to shiver from the cold. We stayed dressed as we were, but we put our ponchos, which helped us to retain our body heat. It was really crazy weather—one minute insufferable heat, the next a freezing, torrential rain.

A short distance south of Cairo, the rain stopped as suddenly as it had begun. The sun popped out and the heat and humidity engulfed us again. Even though we didn't make many miles that day, we decided to look for a campsite. Two miles south of Cairo we went ashore on a sandbar named Angelo Towhead. There wasn't one speck of shade anywhere near us. Just hot sand. It was obvious that the squall didn't reach this far south.

While unloading the canoe, we found that just about everything we owned was soaking wet, including Stinky, the "Commander in Chief." Had he been "wringable" that would have been the easiest and quickest way to dry him out. Worry not about Stinky, he rolled in the dry sand, and then shook himself so hard that he tipped over. By doing this several times, he was able to get rid of most of the water in his fur. Soon he began to look like a kitten again, instead of a drowned white rat. After we pitched the tent, Lou went off to the tree line to cut some "shade brush." Meantime, I began sorting through the pile of wet clothing, cots, knapsacks, camping gear, and food supply. Even the clothes in the supposedly waterproof knapsacks were wet. Some of the labels on the canned goods had gotten so wet they fell off. It was apparent that we would have a few surprise meals in the future.

Of all the stuff in the canoe, only our cameras remained dry, and then because they were kept in waterproof bags.

We built a small lean-to for shade. Every protruding stick and twig held an item of clothing (or whatever) hung out to dry. We turned the canoe over and covered the entire length of it with wet clothes and towels. We put the cots in the sun to dry out. Our campsite certainly didn't look like a proper one. It looked more like a haphazard garage sale set up by two river tramps. We definitely looked the part. By now we were deeply tanned and our clothes began to have a bleached out and tattered look, and were none too clean. It was fortunate that we had made camp early, since it took a few hours for everything to dry. In the evening our rain-soaked guns were broken down, cleaned, and oiled.

As the sun began to go down, our usual uninvited guests joined us—mosquitoes!!! They were nightly guests from the very first day. Into the tent we went, as they were especially thick on this night. We spent the remainder of the evening studying the river maps by lantern light. In spite of all the adversities, we had reached and passed (by two miles) goal number three—Cairo, Illinois.

Cairo is a city completely surrounded by levees and embankments. It's virtually an island city between the Mississippi River and the Ohio. The city is located at the very southern tip of Illinois, with Missouri to the west and Kentucky to the east. It was lucky for us that we had stocked up on needed supplies in Cape Girardeau, because there were no piers, wharves, docks, etc., according to the river map. On the Ohio side we would have had to paddle up the river a few miles to reach docking accommodations.

CHAPTER 26

The Fish

THE NEXT DAY WE began using the second map book, which would take us to New Orleans. It was a very awkward book to use, especially in a canoe. It was twice the size of the first one, thirteen by nineteen inches, very thick, and made of extra heavy paper. But it was a map that was very detailed in every respect. It even marked sunken and exposed boat wrecks. It also included extensive land areas on both sides of the river.

As we passed the mouth of the Ohio River, a young man was entering the Mississippi from the Ohio on a small raft. He waved to us and thinking he needed help we paddled toward him. As we met in the middle of the Mississippi, the two very different crafts were joined together and allowed to just drift down the river while we visited. It turned out that he didn't need any help but was rather interested in seeing a canoe on the Mississippi, a very rare sight. We, of course, were surprised to see a rafter, especially one alone. He was also surprised to see two women in the canoe. It appeared to us that he was somewhat skeptical that we had actually begun our canoe trip in northern Minnesota, and were still alive and well. He had started his journey at Cincinnati. His wife had gone along with him, but he didn't think it was a good idea for her to continue on down the Mississippi. Much too dangerous for a woman! When they reached Cairo, she returned to Cincinnati by bus. We felt it was more dangerous for him to be alone, than it was for we two women on the river. During our visit, not once did he disclose his destination, nor did we ask him. We thought that if he wanted us to know he would tell us. After a short visit, we paddled on down the river, leaving him adrift in the middle of the Mississippi. We often wondered if he ever got to where he was going. He had very little camping equipment and supplies. He maybe wondered about us, too.

After leaving the rafter we had 875 miles to go to reach New Orleans. Our target for the day was not a city or small town, but rather paddling at least forty to forty-five miles before camping for the night. Towards noon we decided to take a shore break on a sandbar that might provide just a little shade. The heat of the day was building up. It was going to be another very hot day. Stinky needed a break, too. He had spent most of the morning under the tarp, out of the sun. Lying on the bottom of the canoe was the coolest place for him to be on a hot day. The river's water kept the bottom of the canoe from getting too warm.

We finally gave up looking for a sandbar with shade, and pulled into the first solid bar we saw. As soon as Stinky was put on shore he waded into the river until the water was deep enough to wet his belly.

Lou and I waded in and sat down in waist deep water. There was no need to take off the few clothes we had on, since they would dry on our bodies within an hour. Even though the water was so dirty (you couldn't see through six inches of it), it was exhilarating to cool off, even just a little.

After a good soaking in the river, we continued on, since we still had about twenty miles to go in order to meet our goal for the day. This day was one of many, many more to come when it would be almost unbearable to be in the sun all day. Again, we oftentimes soaked our sponges in the river and then squeezed the water over our heads. Wherever it went from there felt good, even if the coolness lasted for only a short time. We smelled like the river.

Things were going well for us when suddenly, without warning, the canoe again came to a abrupt halt. Here we were, almost in the very middle of the river—which was very wide at this point—and found that we were grounded on a large submerged sandbar. We could hardly believe that we could become grounded in the middle of the river.

By getting out of the canoe, it reduced the weight enough that we could push and pull it in an effort to find deeper water. Lou was at the bow, measuring the water depth with her paddle. We knew that the sandbar could end at any time, and then there would be many feet of water. Sometimes the canoe would float freely for a few yards, then become grounded again. We'd been struggling with the sandbar for what seemed like a long time, when Lou let out a terrifying cry. In a flash she was back in the canoe and pointing at a large black fish that was lying in water so shallow it barely covered its back. The fact that she stepped on it didn't seem to bother it enough to make it swim away. Her fright was the result of stepping, *barefoot*, on a large, slimy, soft object and not knowing it was just a fish. I had never seen a live fish so large, nor had I ever seen Lou move so quickly! The fish had to have been at least five feet long, with a huge, broad head, and long black whiskers. We guessed it to be a Channel Cat, or maybe a Blue Cat fish. Lou poked him a few times with her paddle and he finally swam off. We eventually cleared the sandbar and entered deeper water. This was the last of the few times that we waded barefoot in the river. Never again!

Later in the day, five miles south of Hickman, Kentucky, we found a nice sandbar for camp. We cut scrub trees for a much needed lean-to that we had to drag a couple of hundred yards back to our campsite. That evening after supper, Lou and I took another soaking and bath in the river. Dirty water or not, it cooled us and we actually felt clean even if we weren't. Stinky had long before taken his "belly deep" wade.

That night, in looking at the river map, we found we had 830 more miles to New Orleans. The river was definitely meandering its way to the Gulf. It flowed every direction found on a compass. Sometimes it went straight north, then turned and went south, meaning that we paddled double the distance and wound up at almost the same place we started from. In the area of Kentucky, Tennessee, and Missouri the river is in total control, meandering when and where it wants. We went to bed early; the heat of the day had drained us. Tomorrow would surely be as hot or hotter.

During our time on the river I do not recall that either of us had a health problem that prevented us from hitting the river any day. Personally, I never felt more healthy.

CHAPTER 27

Tempers Flare

As THE HOT DAYS came, one after another, it seemed as if we talked less and less while paddling. What little talk there was, was about the heat or about Stinky. We were both concerned about him and the effect the heat might have on him. Our only hope was that he could handle it without becoming ill. I was worried about him because he spent most of every day under the tarp. It wasn't the coolest place in the world, but it was better than being in the hot sun.

I did a lot of thinking during the long periods of silence between us, which were becoming more frequent. Lou must have too, but we didn't share our thoughts. I don't think we wanted the other to know what was really on our minds. Neither of us wanted to say out loud: "I give up."

After days upon days of heat, rain squalls, severe storms, mosquitoes, and squalid conditions in general, it was getting to me! I felt as if I'd had enough of everything, including the river. In the beginning it was a miserable and fun experience all rolled into one big adventure. Now it was becoming just miserable without the *fun*!

On the plus side, we hadn't had any personal injuries of any seriousness. Stinky appeared to be taking the heat in stride, even though he spent much of a hot day under the tarp. We had been in a number of life-threatening situations and managed to survive. I wondered: Was it just plain luck? Was it because we were experienced and tough enough to survive? Or was it because "Someone" was looking after us? I wondered, too, if Lou felt as I did. If she did, we both were too stubborn to admit defeat to the other. I think her thoughts were a duplication of mine. I didn't want to be responsible for calling it quits and ending the journey before its time, and then, maybe, later being told "You're the one who wanted to quit."

It wasn't only the elements that were eating away at our goal. It was apparent to me that we were getting a little tired of each other, becoming touchy about little things said or done. We'd been on the river for more than 1,300 miles. Ten to twelve hours a day in a seventeen-foot canoe, and at night in a seven-by-seven-foot tent—just the two of us and Stinky ninety-five percent of the time. Our tempers were beginning to fray.

So the days passed, when suddenly, just south of the Kentucky border, we both lost our tempers at the same time—all over a small disagreement as to where we were positioned on the river and where to set up camp. A few strong expletives were thrown back and forth. I just exploded and took the river map, which was on my lap, and flung it into the river! Not one word was said by either of us. We paddled back upriver twenty yards or so and retrieved the map, which was still afloat.

Few words were exchanged between us for the next couple of days. When either of us had to urge to talk, it was to Stinky. He probably wondered: why all the attention and talking to me? Unknown to Stinky and us at the time, he would get even more attention the third day after the map incident.

CHAPTER 28

Stinky Disappears

O<small>N THE NIGHT OF</small> the second day of silence between Lou and me, Stinky went to the tent door to be let out. It was an unusual request on his part. I was hesitant to let him go, but as he became more insistent I had no choice but to let him out. I stood by the tent door waiting for him to return. When he didn't come back after a few minutes, I began calling him. Still no Stinky. I woke up Lou, and we both went out with flashlights and hunted for him for a good hour without seeing hide nor hair of our much loved kitten.

We built up a new campfire, hoping he'd see or smell it and come home to the tent. Stinky would sometimes wander a short distance from our campsite in the daytime. But never before did he ever leave the immediate campsite after dark. We sat around the campfire until 3 A.M. taking turns calling for him. And still no Stinky! The absence of the kitten prompted us to talk to each other again. Like old times. Apologizes were exchanged and the animosity and anger dissipated. We were friends again, because of the absence of Stinky.

All we talked about was Stinky, his whereabouts, and would we ever see him again. There were reminisces of his first few weeks with us, and his steadfast attachment to both of us. He favored neither of us over the other. His love for us was equal. I always had a cat or two, and kittens during my childhood and at various times during my adult life. *Never* did I have a kitten like Stinky.

It is often believed that cats are very independent and do not want or need human companionship. NOT TRUE! We found Stinky as a very young and possibly wild kitten. He lived in close contact with us twenty-four hours a day for weeks, and as a result he bonded with both of us, just like a puppy.

There were times when I think he thought he *was* a puppy or dog. Whenever a new campsite was established and the tent pitched, he would oftentimes lie in front of the tent door as if guarding our new home. His adjustment to our lifestyle was unbelievable. We talked of him as one might of a missing child. How we did miss him! The worry over Stinky began to turn into grief, as we didn't think we would ever see him again. We talked about all the things that could have happened to him along the river bank, or in the nearby bush. A feral cat could have done him in. But, since we hadn't heard a cat fight, we counted that possibility out. A snake might have zapped him, or maybe he was stuck in some muck along the river—both distinct possibilities. It was very possible that he was up in a tree and unable to get down. We decided that if he didn't show up by 6 A.M. we would explore the river's shore and the trees near our campsite in hopes of finding him. If we couldn't find him by mid-morning, we would just have to leave without him. It was a possibility we didn't even want to think about.

We put some more wood on the fire, still hoping that Stinky might see or smell it and come home. Both of us were tired physically and mentally from the extra-long day and worrying over Stinky. It was way past time for us to get some needed sleep, if possible. We left the tent door unzipped on the floor and for about eight inches, so he could get in when and if he returned. It was not a wise thing to do, as a snake could crawl in, but we did it for Stinky. By this time we'd do most anything to have our kitten back.

I didn't think either one of us would sleep very soundly. Apparently we did, because when we woke shortly after seven o'clock, there he was, lying on the foot end of Lou's cot. At that moment we were probably the happiest two women on the entire river. Never would we have to worry about having left him behind, or wonder about what happened to him that night, had he not returned. As it turned out, I will still always wonder what really happened to him "that night."

When he felt us petting him and heard us talking to him, the "purr motor" kicked in. But, he made no attempt to stand. He was lying on his right side, with the right paw sort of wrapped around the right side of his head. As I began petting his head, which he usually liked, he pulled away from my hand. It was obvious there was something wrong with him.

Finally he lifted us his head and looked at us. We couldn't believe what we saw: His right eye was swollen more than twice the size of the left eye. (Cats have very large eyes in comparison to their body size.) His eye was almost as large as a ping-pong ball. It looked as if it were ready to pop right out of his head. It was so large he was unable

67

to blink or close it, and the pupil covered the entire eye. The iris wasn't even visible. And he appeared to be in extreme pain.

The only pain medicine we had was aspirin. It was either that or nothing. We made up some powered milk and crushed an aspirin into it. Stinky was thirsty and hungry, so there was no problem in getting him to drink it. The aspirin would also reduce the fever we suspected he had. We didn't know it then, but that aspirin could have killed him. Lucky for him and us, it didn't. After a couple of days and more aspirin and milk, his eye returned to normal size without any evidence of permanent damage.

We never determined for sure how his eye was injured or why he didn't come to us when we called for him over and over again most of the night. One thing was certain: He was stung or bitten by something very poisonous—possibly a spider, mud hornet, or some other insect unknown to us. In any event, we believed that he must have lost consciousness for a time, and was probably unable to walk for even longer. Whatever bit or stung him, the poison was not only in his eye, but in his entire body, as he had difficulty walking for several hours.

It wasn't until late morning when we left the campsite. It was the first time we ever had to carry Stinky down to the river and put him into the canoe. He slept most of the day under the tarp, recovering from his near fatal accident.

CHAPTER 29

A Winding River

As soon as Stinky recovered from his near-fatal accident, he pursued his usual activities. Lying on the bow of the canoe, and, when on shore, chasing one of his "river toys"— dragon flies, moths, or crawling insects of any kind. I think he learned which insects were "fair game," as he was never bitten or stung for the rest of the journey.

Stinky never owned a store-bought toy. In fact, we never even thought of buying him one. We did, however, fashion various things for him to play with. They were made of either a piece of paper, cardboard, or a leaf from a bush. They were tied to a string, which either Lou or I would pull for him to chase. He needed the exercise after being in the canoe for many hours each day. He knew that evenings were playtime for him.

Our days were happy again. We still had our Stinky. We talked, laughed, and put up with the heat, storms, and mosquitoes with laughter in our hearts.

For most of the last seven hundred miles, the river meandered in every direction found on a compass. It seemed as if we couldn't really advance any distance before doubling back. Had we been able to portage the dog legs, we could have saved miles and miles of paddling. But portaging was next to impossible. The portage route would be swampy and infested with snakes and insects. It could also include portaging over revetments and levees. Also, we probably would expend more physical energy portaging than we would in paddling. As an example of the winding river, at Mile 905 it is almost unbelievable. The river map showed explicitly how the river shaped the land as well as the people who lived on or near the river. To the north of the river is the State of Missouri. To the east and south, Tennessee, and in the middle of the dog leg, Kentucky. Then to the west, Missouri again. The residents of Tennessee and Kentucky who are in the middle or near the middle of the dog leg may never know from one year to the next which state they live in, due to the river changing its course. There are many such dog legs or open-ended loops of the river from Cairo all the way to New Orleans.

As we were passing Fulton County, Kentucky, on the west side of the above described dog leg, we noticed smoke rising from a small hill near the river. Several boats were pulled up on the shore. Along with the smoke coming from the hill we could hear music and the voices of a number of people. Always eager to talk to the natives that we met along the river, we paddled up to the shore. The aroma that came wafting down the hill smelled familiar, but we couldn't determine exactly what it was.

As we climbed the hill, the aroma became stronger and more distinct. SMOKING HAMS!! A group of people were making hickory-smoked hams. When they saw us and Stinky, a group of children came running to meet not Lou and me, but instead Stinky!! As we approached the adults, we introduced ourselves, and Stinky too. They were the first people we had met who knew nothing of us, which in a sense was a pleasant surprise. They had a pop stand of sorts and we each bought a bottle of root beer which we think was homemade.

In talking to some of the adults present, we found that the smoking of hams was done at this location several times a year by local families. There were about a dozen hams smoking over beds of hickory coals. They offered to sell us a ham, but since they only sold whole hams, we had to decline. We didn't have any refrigeration and not even ice to keep a ten-pound ham from spoiling. We left the ham smokers with only the smell of ham. But we did have an opportunity to visit with the locals.

CHAPTER 30

Life with a Kitten

OFTENTIMES, DAYS WOULD GO by without our conversing with other people. Yes, there were three of us, counting Stinky, but it can still be lonely. Before we started our voyage, we had attempted to find two other women to join us. There were several who were interested, but most had little or no canoe experience. After we explained to them all that would be involved, including the possible dangers, they decided canoeing the Mississippi was not their idea of a vacation. In hindsight, we found that we had enough difficulties in taking care of ourselves, let alone two inexperienced canoeists.

From the very beginning to the end of the voyage, many individuals and groups helped us, even coming to our rescue on more than one occasion. Had there been four of us *and* a kitten, I wonder now whether we would have been so easily accommodated and offered assistance.

Stinky was never denied accommodations, be it a motel, private home, towboat or hotel, except for once in Vicksburg, Mississippi. For the most part he was a well-behaved kitten. As a child I always had a cat or two and kittens. But I had never lived so closely with a cat or kitten, twenty-four hours a day for over two months. Living closely *with* a kitten is far different from just having one. Believe me, it was quite an experience. I might also say a pleasant one. I probably learned more about kittens during those two months than I had ever dreamed possible. It is commonly believed that kittens and cats are very independent, self-sufficient, and do not need a lot of human contact. That they don't miss their human owner(s) when they are absent. And, finally that they don't bond to their owners as most dogs do.

Nothing could be further from the truth. Stinky demonstrated all of this to be a myth. He became part of us and very dependent. He, after a few weeks, knew the full routine—making camp, breaking camp, when to eat, sleep, or play. There were times when he fell out of the canoe, but he would immediately swim back to us. He knew that he had two homes, the canoe and the tent. Nearly every evening the tent was pitched at a new location, but that didn't matter to him. As soon as it was up, he would lie in front of it. Instead of a guard dog, we had a *guard kitten*. Home to Stinky was any place, as long as Lou or I were there with him. In the mornings when he saw the canoe being loaded, he would sit next to it, patiently waiting to be put in. He made sure he wasn't going to be forgotten and left behind.

As time we on, he lost all fear of water. In fact, he enjoyed a swim or a wade, and even liked to lie in the "run-offs" flowing into the river. After a hot day in the canoe, he found this to be a good way to cool off.

We didn't realize, when we first found him, how much his presence would add to the trip. Nor did we know how attached to him we would become. I think we had more concern for him than we did for each other. Had we lost our "Captain Stinky" for one reason or another, it would have been devastating to both Lou and me. Every day seemed to revolve around him, his welfare and whereabouts. The journey would not have been the same without Stinky.

Chapter 31

Tornado

LATE IN THE AFTERNOON of the "smoked hams day" the sky to the southwest took on an ominous appearance. Dark, low hanging, heavy clouds were moving quickly in our direction. The day had been hot and humid, without a breath of wind. Suddenly we felt a light and cool breeze, and we could see lightning and hear thunder in the far distance. Time to go ashore!

We had to find a place to camp on the west shore of the river, which would give us some protection from the impending storm, and we had to be quick about it. Finally we found a small, narrow sandbar with a high dirt and grass bank behind it. The bank would give us additional protection against any high winds that might blow in. We still didn't know how severe the storm would be; our little radio couldn't pick up any radio stations because of the incessant static.

The tent was pitched more quickly than ever before. That was one big, big mistake, one that we never repeated when a storm was coming toward us. We pulled up the canoe near the tent and anchored it the best we could into the solid dirt bank. We would make no preparations for supper until the storm passed. The little time we had left was used to stash away our equipment and supplies. We took the little motor off the motor mount and laid next to the canoe, instead of under it. That was mistake number two. At the time, we felt it was perfectly safe next to the canoe. In our haste, we neglected a number of other items, the most important being our paddles.

It was beginning to look like the storm would be a dandy. The sky took on a greenish tint and the cool wind we had suddenly stopped. Not a leaf stirred. It was dead silent except for the thunder and crack of lightning in the distance. The black, menacing clouds were swirling at a fast pace, coming in our direction. It seemed as if they were almost touching the ground. It was then that we heard a low roaring sound, not unlike that of a train. We knew then it wasn't just a thunderstorm, but a tornado, and it was heading right for us. We quickly stuffed Stinky under the canoe. His animal instincts told him to stay put. Lou and I threw ourselves flat on our stomachs next to the dirt bank. We put our arms over and behind our heads and waited. The wait was terrifying. My heart pounded so hard it felt as if it was in my throat. We didn't have to wait for long . . .

Suddenly the "train" was upon us. We couldn't see the destruction, but hear it we did. Fortunately the tornado had leap-frogged over us and all we got, which was more than enough, was a tremendous down-draft from the fierce wind and buckets of cold rain after it passed. It was all over as quickly as it came.

After the wind and rain subsided I got to my feet and found Stinky digging himself out from under the canoe. The canoe had been turned over and was completely covered with sand, except for the bottom. The motor was buried. That turned out to be bad news. All I could see of Lou was her butt and a slight hump where her head appeared to be. As soon as she got up and shook the sand off of herself, we made an assessment of damages.

The tent was smashed to the ground and covered with sand, along with everything else. Stinky was still digging himself out from under the canoe, and with a little help from us he was soon out. There wasn't one grain of sand on him. He had been well protected. Lou and I had sand inside our clothing; even the pockets of our shorts were filled with sand. We had sand in our ears, eyes, mouth, and packed into our hair. Off came all of our clothes and into the river we went to wash the sand out of us. It was then that we saw, floating down the river, brush and trees of all sizes that the tornado had uprooted. I thought, "Aren't we lucky! We could very well have been out there with all the debris deposited by the tornado." Lucky, too, we still had our canoe.

We then took an inventory of our property. At first we thought we still had everything, even though it was scattered here and there. Then, we suddenly realized that two very important items were not to be seen—our *paddles*! We started a desperate search. After kicking sand for what seemed like ages, we finally found them, buried some distance from where we had left them. Now everything was accounted for, but not all was in usable condition. When the tent went down, the T-bar across the top of the tent broke and the sharp metal edge of the bar tore a slit more than a foot long in the top of the tent.

It was much too late to attempt to repair it. It would have to wait until morning. Our wooden food box, not being air-tight, was full of sand, and there was sand in some of the boxed food. This, too, would have to wait until morning. It would soon be dark and we hadn't had anything to eat since noon. Neither of us was very hungry. I guess the excitement and fear of the tornado wiped away all pangs of hunger—except for Stinky. He followed us around like a little trailer, wondering when we were going to eat.

After rummaging around in the canvas bag that held our canned goods, we found a can without a label, one of several left from the rainstorm a few days before. In opening it we found it was pork and beans. Not too bad for a "surprise supper." We added a small can of wieners to the beans. Biscuits and a pot of coffee completed the impromptu supper. Stinky ate his share and then sat next to the smashed down tent, probably wondering when we were going to put it up. After supper we sat around the fire and discussed our predicament, especially the tent. How were we to sleep in a flattened tent? We also talked about how lucky all three of us were to have escaped injury.

We restaked the tent, so that the floor would be tight. That night we slept, or tried to sleep, under the flapping canvas. There was a slight breeze, which was good, otherwise we would have cooked under what was once a tent. Stinky slept under our cots, so he didn't have to deal with the flapping canvas all night. Prior to this day, we had seen tornadoes but none right on top of us. Nor had we ever felt so vulnerable.

Most of the next morning was spent getting rid of the sand in every piece of equipment we owned—food parcels, knapsacks, cooking utensils, and the little motor, which we found would not start. We sewed up the rip in the tent with heavy thread. We had a can of fiberglass and hardener for canoe repair, and decided it might also help in tent repair. We spread a liberal amount over the mended tear to make it waterproof and give it strength. In subsequent rainstorms it never leaked a drop. The T-bar was another matter. It was a hollow aluminum conduit pipe, which had broken at its weakest point, right where the vertical pipe fit into the bar. We cut a small, seven-foot-long sapling and every night lashed it to the T-bar to hold it together. It was a temporary solution. We had a saggy tent and knew it would never withstand wind of any degree. We had to find someone to fix the T-bar, but didn't know who, when, or where.

74

By noon we were able to leave our "camp of devastation." We paddled for several miles before we were free of floating debris from the tornado. Stinky was entranced by the floating objects in the river, so thick in places that I think he thought we were on land and he could just jump out and walk around. We had to fish him out only one time. He learned his lesson.

It was cloudy, so we had a comfortable day on the river. By 6 P.M. we found a well-protected sandbar on the west shore. From then on, we would forever be wary of an impending storm or tornado. Whenever possible, we tried to camp on the west side of the river which was safer than the east. The river here appeared to be cleaner than usual, so we took a swim and *again* washed our hair, which still had sand in it. When we ate, we found sand in our food. Some of it couldn't be seen, but our teeth would tell us it was there. We didn't have a "sandless" meal for days.

That evening, we tried to get the motor in running order. We never knew when it might be needed. We cleaned the carburetor in a haphazard fashion, since neither of us knew much about them, except that they were important in making an engine run. We installed a new spark plug and filled it with gas, but it still wouldn't start. It sounded like it wanted to, but it just wouldn't "pop." Our efforts to adjust the carburetor were of no help. Trying to get it to run appeared to be a lost cause, so we gave up. Now we would need help for the motor, too.

That night we slept fitfully. A slight wind came up and I expected the tent to come down any minute. Stinky slept under our cots. He could hear the creaking of the sapling bending and maybe he, too, thought the tent would fall on him. We got up about 4 A.M. and were hardly out of the tent, when down it went!

By 5:30 A.M. we were on the river, and even that early in the morning we knew it was going to be another hot, muggy day. Later in the morning, we came upon a man fishing. He was in quite a large john boat with a nice big umbrella shielding him from the sun. I thought how nice it must be, to be out in the middle of the river without the incessant sun beating on you.

As we approached him, he waved us over to his boat. As we neared, I couldn't see any fish poles, and decided he must not be fishing as we had first thought. But, fishing he was—with a "trot line."

He had one-quart metal oil cans which were sealed air-tight. They were strung out on one long line and tied about ten feet apart. Attached to each can was a fish line and on the end of each line was a large treble hook buried into a porous bag, the size of an orange, and filled with putrid chicken entrails. He was, we found out, fishing for catfish.

We told him of our encounter with a tornado the day before, about the wrecked tent and the motor that wouldn't run. We also needed fresh drinking water. He told us that downriver a few miles there was a logging camp, and that we could get drinking water there and even help for the motor and T-bar repair. Our visit with the fisherman was educational and informative. We learned all about cat fishing and, we hoped, how to find some help with our repair problems.

CHAPTER 32
The Logging Camp

SHORTLY AFTER LEAVING THE fisherman, we heard the faint sounds of singing. As we moved on downriver they became clearer—all male voices. Rounding a bend, we saw African-Americans hand-loading huge logs onto barges. The heat was oppressive and there was not one wisp of wind that day, and yet these men were singing. I believe the singing had something to do with the rhythm required in loading the logs. It required three or four men to handle each log, and they had to work in unison. We passed by the barges they were loading and pulled into a nearby pier.

Lou stayed with Stinky and the canoe while I went to the main buildings of the logging camp with the motor. As I approached the buildings it became apparent to me that we were unlikely to find any help for our motor, and maybe not even drinking water. But, as the saying goes, nothing ventured, nothing gained! It appeared to be a very old logging camp. Most of the buildings were shacks, looking as if they were ready to fall down. These included the living quarters for the men of the camp and their families. Some shacks were missing doors. None had glass in the windows. As I walked past them, I could see that newspapers served as wallpaper. The living quarters were nothing more than one- or two-room hovels. Never in my life had I seen living conditions for humans as squalid as these.

Nearly all the women were poorly dressed, barefoot, and in dire need of any small comforts a human should be expected to have. The number of flies and mosquitoes was intolerable. They were on everything, be it dead or alive. The children were scantly dressed because of the heat and probably for the lack of clothing. Their bodies were covered with welts from insect bites.

After questioning several women, I was directed to the man in charge of the camp. The "man" turned out to be a boy of sixteen. He told me his father was the camp boss, but since he was gone that day, he was in charge of the camp. After telling him of the motor problem, he suggested that the camp's mechanic might be able to help me.

The repair shop and the mechanic were both total disasters! The shop was a rundown shack in complete disarray. It looked more like a junk shop. The mechanic was an elderly white man who was somewhat intoxicated. I then questioned whether I should request his help. My better judgement told me NO! But I was desperate for help, and for help I asked.

I explained the motor problem to him. He told me he knew all about outboard motors. He could fix it. He began to tear the motor down, but every few minutes he'd sit back down in an old, worn rocker to have a few sips of beer. After a short time it became apparent to me that he was becoming very intoxicated and totally incapable of working on the motor. It was also evident that he knew very little about outboard motors when he asked me where the spark plug was located. At that point, I politely suggested that we put it back together since it was a hopeless case. By that time he was unable to use a screwdriver because of his many sips of beer. Much to my surprise he agreed. I was glad about that, since I didn't particularly want to get into an argument with a drunken man. It ended up that I alone put the motor back together as best I could. Admittedly, I had a few leftover screws, etc. and these I put into my pocket for later use. As a matter of courtesy and goodwill I gave him a few dollars for his feeble efforts.

As I was walking back to the canoe I encountered the boy in charge of the camp. I told him I didn't have any luck in getting the motor repaired, and we were in dire need of getting the T-bar of the tent repaired. He said that a towboat was coming about midnight to pick up the loaded barges. They would be going downriver to Greenville, Mississippi. Maybe we could hitch a ride and travel with them until the tent and motor were repaired. He suggested that we go downriver about half a mile to wait for the towboat, since it might be dangerous for us to wait near the logging camp. We would be able to see the lights of the boat down there, as well as hear it coming, and we would have plenty of time to come back upriver to contact the captain of the tow.

I then asked him if there was any drinking water to be had. "Ya, over there's a barrel by the shed, you take what you need." I looked where he pointed and the "shed" was in far better shape than the living quarters for the workers. I got our empty GI water can and filled it. I then thought, this water has a familiar odor. Later we found we couldn't use the water for anything, as it was tainted with gasoline. Apparently the workers had no choice—drink it or go without!

When I got to the canoe I told Lou of the boy's advice, and we decided to do as he suggested. It was late afternoon when we left the camp and went downriver to wait for the towboat.

Chapter 33

Towboat Assistance

We chose a sandbar on the west side of the river for a waiting site. It was on the same side of the river as the logging camp. We unloaded only some items we thought we would need for what we hoped would be a short stay.

There wasn't a drop of shade to be had. The tree line was far from the river, too far for us to get material to build a lean-to for protection from the ferocious sun. In looking at the river map, we found that we were in Arkansas. Across the river was the southern part of Tennessee.

Soon after we arrived at the sandbar, two fisherman appeared at the scene. They couldn't imagine what were doing sitting on a sandbar in the middle of nowhere. After telling them of all our problems and mishaps they offered to try to fix the engine. They did find all the places for the extra screws and nuts, but still the engine would not run. During the visit we told them of our plans to contact the incoming towboat that night. They told us, in so many words, that it was dangerous for us to be so close to the logging camp. But we had no choice other than to stay where we were, in sight of the camp and barges. The lights of the incoming towboat that night would be a signal for us to go back upriver to get the help we needed.

For the rest of the afternoon we sat sweltering on the hot sand and in the ever-present hot sun. Stinky lay in the shade of the canoe, which we had pulled well onto shore. Even there he was warmer than he wanted to be. Every so often, he'd wade into the river for a drink and to cool off.

After supper, we gathered wood for a fire to ward off the hordes of mosquitoes that were bound to show up at sundown. We had to have enough wood to last until at least midnight. The gathering had to be done in daylight, since we weren't about to look for wood after dark. After about an hour, our wood pile had grown large enough to last throughout our stay on the sandbar. As dusk turned into night, we spent our time swatting mosquitoes and looking at our watches . . . 8 P.M. . . . 9 P.M. . . . 10 P.M. It seemed to take forever for midnight to arrive.

Midnight came and went and still no towboat. We began to think we might be the butts of a cruel joke. Maybe we spent the late afternoon and all night on a hot, mosquito-infested sandbar for nothing! We began to talk about setting up the tent and forgetting about the towboat entirely. The mosquitoes were just about driving us bananas. But then, shortly before 1 A.M., we spotted bright lights near the logging camp. Surely, that must be the towboat! We could hear its engines and hear the shouting of men.

The canoe was quickly loaded up with the few items that we had removed. Stinky sat in the middle of the canoe on top of the tarp. He was very likely enjoying being on the river at night. Nighttime is usually cats' time to roam. Because of a strong river current, we decided to tow the canoe along shore by ropes. Lou had the kerosene lantern at the stern. I used a flashlight at the bow to see ahead and along the shore. We waded close to shore with just enough depth to float the canoe, ever on the lookout for rattlers and cottonmouths. In less than an hour we were adjacent to the towboat. With the lantern on top of the tarp, we began paddling toward it.

As we approached, we saw a man standing on an upper deck shouting directions to the men on the barges and those on the towboat. We decided that he had to be the captain. We stayed about thirty yards away from the tow and barges to keep out of all the activity. After things calmed down a bit, the man, who indeed was the captain, spotted us in the canoe. His first words were, "What the hell are you two doing here?" Before we could even muster an answer, he continued, "Damnation! You two boys get the hell out of here before you get run over and sunk!"

We responded as quickly as we could—before he could continue. We told him, we were *not* boys, but instead two women. When he heard that, he really blew his stack! With abundant, effusive cursing, he told us we had no business being on the river, especially in the dark of night. The river, at any time, was a dangerous place for two women. At that point, we had to agree with him.

He finally got around to asking who we were and why we were on the river in the wee hours of the morning and in a CANOE of all things! We told him that we were two school teachers on vacation. That information again set him off! With an abundance of expletives, he said he could think of a lot of better places for a vacation! He got that right again, as we were beginning to think so, too.

It began to cross our minds that this captain may not be of any help to us, after all. We finally got up the courage to tell him of our problems and a desperate need for assistance. He instantly became a mellow, polite "southern gentleman." He then offered to help "the damsels in distress." He told us to paddle out into the river away from the towboat and barges. We were to wait there. After the barges were all lined up to move south they would stop and pick us up. It was now nearly 2 A.M. We paddled out to the designated area. Because of the current, we had to keep pushing north to keep ourselves opposite the towboat. The lit lantern was left on top of the tarp to make sure they would see us.

After what seemed like hours, we could at last see and hear the barges coming toward us. They were linked together, four barges wide and eight barges long. They were being pushed by the little towboat that we could barely see. The whole thing looked like a huge monster coming at us.

We knew the barges would be pushed past us in order for the towboat to pick us up. We certainly felt vulnerable alongside the enormous barges. Very slowly they passed by us, and the next thing we knew the towboat was at our side. The captain was on deck along with two deck hands.

"Well," he said, "are you ladies ready to board my boat?" We were more than ready to board his boat! Most of our equipment and supplies were handed up to the men on the deck. With the canoe nearly empty we were given a hand up onto the deck. Stinky had been harnessed and leashed. I held him in my arms as I was helped up. The men pulled the canoe onto the deck with the ropes that were on the bow and stern. The captain shook our hands and welcomed us aboard. He was a nice looking man, about sixty years old, with a neatly trimmed white beard. Now, he looked and acted like the fatherly type.

It required a lot of maneuvering of the barges and towboat to pick us up.

The captain certainly was determined to offer a helping hand to us two damsels in distress. Never again did we curse the towboats and barges that so often seemed to threaten us on the river.

CHAPTER 34

Weatherwood Vacation

As soon as we and all of our stuff were safely aboard, he led us to a two-bunk guest cabin. Fortunately we had the foresight to bring a small box of sand for Stinky. This time he didn't use it to play in. Instead he used it for its intended purpose shortly after he got settled in. By now it was nearly 3 A.M. All three of us were more than weary, just plain "dead beat."

As the captain left, he said that breakfast was served from 6 to 7 A.M. Not having an alarm clock, we didn't wake until 9 A.M. Stinky's "head alarm," we discovered, was not infallible. He, as well as Lou and I, hadn't had even so much as a catnap in almost twenty-four hours. No one could be more embarrassed than we were, missing our breakfast appointment!

As we entered the mess room the cook greeted us with a smile, "I knew you would oversleep. What would you like for breakfast?"

We didn't want to be picky, anything would be fine with us. Both of us answered at the same time, "Anything you have." It turned out to be a breakfast fit for a king: Bacon, eggs, toast, juice, coffee, and grits. The grits were new to us. To me, they tasted a little like cream of wheat. It was the best meal we'd had in some time. Each of us put aside a little of our breakfast for Stinky. After a lengthy conversation with the cook, we came away much more knowledgeable about towboats and barges. Our respect for them and their work increased substantially.

The captain of a towboat must pass rigorous tests before being licensed as a captain. Most captains are older men with considerable experience from the ground up. From what I can remember: A towboat has a captain, a first mate, an engineer who is in charge of the boat's engine performance, and a cook, who sometimes has an assistant or mess boy. The hands can number five or more, depending on the number of barges to be pushed and the number of days on the river. Most important is the amount of cargo to be loaded or unloaded. One large barge can carry loads many times that of a railroad car. From what I observed, being a deck hand is dangerous and hard work. All the crews I spoke with were kind and polite, real gentlemen.

Until our meeting with the cook, we were unaware that the towboats had names. We learned that we were on the *Weatherwood,* owned by U.S. Gypsum. Its destination was Greenville, Mississippi, about 230 miles downriver. We didn't know it then, but we were to be guests of the *Weatherwood* until it reached Greenville. We were in for two and a half to three days of shade, good food, and no canoeing. A real REST.

Now we were finally on vacation! All our meals were prepared, and they were free, as was our cabin. We spent some of our time visiting with the captain and crew members. But most of our time was passed just sitting in lawn chairs, pleasantly viewing the river scenery. This, I thought, is the way to spend a summer on the "Father of Waters."

Stinky was with us most of the time, except for his usual early afternoon nap. With his ability to adapt, he never once posed a problem. When on deck he was always harnessed and leashed. He was almost always sitting on one of our laps, taking in all the activity on the boat and the scenery passing by.

Early afternoon on the first day, the engineer came to us and offered his help in getting the motor running and repairing the tent's T-bar. Within twenty-four hours the T-bar was repaired and the motor was back in running order. The motor just needed a good cleaning to get the sand out of it and some carburetor adjustment. The T-bar was welded and reinforced with a band of metal and riveted. Our problems were all solved by one kindly engineer. Before reaching Greenville, stops were made at Memphis, Tennessee, and Helena, Arkansas, to drop off some of the barges. There was no opportunity for us to disembark.

CHAPTER 35

Greenville, Mississippi

U NFORTUNATELY, AFTER FORTY YEARS, I cannot remember the captain's name or that of the engineer. Nevertheless, their helpfulness and concern for our safety will never be forgotten.

Early afternoon of the third day we were on the *Weatherwood,* she pulled into the Greenville harbor. After tying off the barges, the captain eased her into her home port berth. Just as we began preparing to leave the towboat, the engineer came to us and told us that we were invited to his home for supper and an overnight stay. He said he'd call his wife. She was looking forward to meeting us and Stinky. More accommodations—this was unbelievable! We readily accepted the invitation, and a short time later his wife arrived to take us to their home.

The canoe, our gear, and equipment were left on the towboat. All would be perfectly safe until the next day when we planned to leave Greenville. Stinky hadn't been in a vehicle in some time, but he acted as if a car ride was a daily routine. Their home was air-conditioned, which was a pleasure beyond description. It felt (after many days) so good to be out of the oppressive heat, if only for a day.

Later in the afternoon, since neither of us had ever been to Greenville, we were offered a tour of the city and a shopping expedition. We couldn't help but notice that there wasn't one tavern or liquor store to be seen. Not at all like Wisconsin. We inquired as to how and where one would purchase a bottle of brandy. The engineer's wife told us that Mississippi was technically a "dry state," but that she would take us out in the country, to a place where we could buy whatever we wanted.

After leaving the city limits and driving on a bumpy, gravel road, we stopped in front of a small, rundown building which seemed to be in the middle of nowhere. It was at the intersection of two roads. There were no other buildings in the area to be seen. A very desolate site to say the least. I couldn't believe that this could be a place to obtain a bottle of brandy, way out in the "boonies."

There were no outdoor signs of any sort advertising the establishment. In entering the building, we were in for another surprise! A long counter extending the length of the backbar was the only piece of furniture to be seen. The backbar shelves were empty except for three or four bottles of liquor. It was my guess that they were only samples of the kinds of liquor available. A bottle of brandy cost us considerably more than we had expected. At the time we didn't know why.

In talking to the hosts we found that these establishments existed in nearly every county in Mississippi. They were not exactly legal, but if the proprietor paid a fine every month to the county, he or she could continue to operate without interference for another month—after which they would be fined again. It's obvious the "dry state" law had a few holes in it.

After a sumptuous supper and a good night's sleep in beds rather than cots or bunks, we were on our way downriver early the next morning. Two crewmen on the towboat helped us put the canoe into the river and load our gear. Thanks to all the wonderful people on the towboat and in Greenville, it was *more* than an ordinary experience.

84

CHAPTER 36

Towboat #2

SINCE THE RIVER TRAFFIC was very heavy as we left the Greenville harbor, we started the motor. We'd only gone a mile or so when it sputtered and died. The engineer on the towboat had told us he did what he could for the engine, but it might need a new part or two. We would just have to try it. It wasn't feasible to go back to the harbor, so out came the paddles. No matter the situation, we would have to do without the motor.

Late that afternoon, about thirty miles south of Greenville, we found a perfect site for camping, a nice sandbar with small saplings and brush nearby for building a lean-to. After being in the shade of the towboat and air-conditioning in Greenville, the return of the sun and unrelenting humidity was tough to handle. Some shade, no matter how little, was imperative for all three of us.

By the time the lean-to was finished, we had what one might call a small oasis, shade and water close by. We had everything we needed, except a motor that worked. Over supper we talked over the perplexing motor problem. Even knowledgeable persons were unable to find the solution. We finally decided that we would have to try seek help from another towboat. The next day we would attempt to stop a towboat that was not pushing barges. If and when we would see a towboat, one us of would paddle out to the main channel and attempt to stop it. This would not be an easy feat, as it takes a while for a towboat to stop, and we would have to see it approaching soon enough in order to be within reaching distance of us. And, last but not least, the towboat may or may not stop to give us help. We flipped a coin and I was designated as the first one to paddle to a towboat—should one stop.

Beginning at daylight the next morning, we took turns watching for free towboats. The canoe was resting on shore, the motor for ballast in the bow. We would paddle kneeling, from a position a third forward from the stern. We had the good fortune to be camped on a straight stretch of shore for some distance north and south, so that with the aid of field glasses we would be able to spot a towboat at quite a distance from our campsite.

From daylight to 8 A.M. more than a dozen tows passed by. All were pushing barges. Hope was fading of seeing a free boat. A short time later, however, we spotted a free towboat coming north. Without any hesitation, I began paddling out to the main river channel. I would have about five or six minutes to try to intercept the towboat. As I neared the part of the river where I believed to be a good place, I noticed the towboat was slowing down. I just sat where I was and began to wave my orange life jacket. Again good fortune was with us. The towboat was coming toward me!

Going at a crawl, it finally stopped a short distance from me. I certainly must have been an oddity, as nearly every crew member was on deck watching me approach their boat. They too, wondered what I was doing on the river, and in a *canoe* of all things. After explaining my situation to a man I presumed to be the captain, I was immediately helped aboard along with the canoe.

I was advised that the towboat would continue moving north. The engineer would do what he could for the motor during that time. In any event, I would return to our campsite by one of two ways, by motor or paddle. I dearly hoped it would be by motor, as paddling a canoe alone is not easy, even with ballast. Lou was back at the campsite with Stinky.

As I was waiting for news of the motor, a crewman told me that a severe storm was raging to the southwest of us. It was hard to believe, as the sun was shining and I could see not a ripple on the river. My first thoughts were of Lou and Stinky! Were they in the middle of the storm?

After about an hour on the towboat, I got the good news! There was nothing wrong with the motor. The gas we used was the problem. The little one-gallon gas can contained nothing but "rotten gas." Since we very rarely purchased gas, it was probably very low in octane, plus there was sand in the can as well as some water due to condensation from the can's exposure to the sun. The sand could have gotten into the can from our clothing or accumulated sand around the can's cap. Neither we nor anyone else prior to this ever suspected that gas was the culprit.

The motor was refilled with fresh gas as well as the one-gallon can. Again, I gained renewed appreciation and thankfulness for the ever-present towboats and their crews.

When I left the towboat to return to our campsite, I was told that I was about thirty to thirty-five miles north of where they had picked me up. My first thoughts centered on the motor. "It sure better run or I would be in DEEP TROUBLE!" After a few minutes the motor seemed to run like it was charmed. That was one thing to be grateful for. With the motor at full speed I could make about ten miles per hour, helped by the river current. After figuring that out, I realized it would take at least three hours to arrive back at the campsite. Then I began to think of Lou and Stinky. Were they in the storm I was told about? What would I find at the campsite? It then came to mind, that this could become a serious situation.

If I encountered any difficulties and did not get back until very late, like the next day—or not at all—they would be stranded without any means of leaving the sandbar. No towboat could leave the main river channel to pick them up. Their only chance would be a stray fisherman, or a pleasure craft. These thoughts caused me to be extra cautious. I had to get back to our campsite without fail.

Lou was alone with Stinky at a campsite in the middle of nowhere. I was alone in a canoe on the "Great River." I have to admit, I was somewhat frightened.

Not sure my calculations were totally correct, I left the main river channel and current about 2 P.M. and traveled close to the west shore. Missing the campsite was definitely not in my plans. A short time later, I noticed leaves, small twigs, and branches floating on the river. It was obvious a storm had to have been in the area, and it must have a storm of violence. Evidence of debris was proof of that.

Luckily, Lou heard a small motor approaching. Sure that it was me, she was on the shore frantically waving her life jacket. I was in total disbelief of the scene: *No tent* to be seen. The lean-to looked like a pile of kindling. The brush growing nearby was smashed flat to the ground. Then I saw Stinky . . . No lives lost. Luck was with us again. If Lou hadn't been on shore, I may well have passed the camp.

Lou had quite a terrifying story to tell. Noticing that the southwest sky began to darken, along with black, surging clouds veined with green, speeding in her direction, she immediately prepared for the worst. Suddenly the light breeze turned into a stiff, cool wind. It took Lou only moments to stuff the tent with all the things (including

Stinky) that might be damaged from the wind and rain that was sure to come. She dropped the tent's T-bar, folding the tent before the wind could tear it down. Using the small army trenching shovel, she dug a hollow out of the sand next to the stand of brush. Lying in the hollow on her stomach, with her arms over the back of her head, she waited for IT to come!

With Lou barely in the hollow, a ferocious wind struck. She could hear the howl of the tornado a short distance away. That was a relief of sorts. She heard cracking brush and the flapping canvas of the downed tent. She then became concerned for Stinky. But nothing could be done. They both had to stay put, and in a relatively short period of time "IT" was gone.

The force of the wind covered Lou and everything we owned with sand, mud, and brush. In a heartbeat, the little oasis was no more! After the storm, Stinky was the first "item" removed from the tent. He, Lou guessed, just hid under the various articles in the tent and was no worse for wear. But, it was quite apparent he was scared out of his wits, as his hackles were raised and his tail was very nearly the size of a rolling pin.

If you've never seen a tornado or even been near one, you can't imagine how frightening it can be. I don't believe there is a word to describe the fear that penetrates your entire body and mind. You'll for-ever be fearful of any kind of impending storm, tornado or not! With both of us having been in severe storms in the past, and not only on the Mississippi, our greatest fear during the journey down the river was a severe storm. We held the utmost respect for them.

After I told Lou of my day on the river, we began to clean up the campsite. Tomorrow was another day. We hoped it would be better than this day.

CHAPTER 37

Coast Guard Rescue

THE NEXT DAY BEGAN bright and sunny with very few clouds afloat, along with the ever-present oppressive heat and humidity. In spite of that, we were happy to be alive and well after nearly a whole day of terror and apprehension. Today, all I wanted was a small umbrella to fend off the glare of the sun. By now, both Lou and I were deeply scorched by the intense sun.

We were now about thirty miles north of Vicksburg, Mississippi, our next intended stop. Earlier, plans were made for us to be guests of the Junior Chamber of Commerce in Vicksburg. If it hadn't been for the towboat's assistance in our time of need, we wouldn't have arrived in time for the planned festivities, the selection of Miss Mississippi for the Miss America Pageant. Even then, there wasn't any certainty we'd arrive at the appointed time. We never knew from one day to the next what we might encounter or what problems might arise. Barring any untoward incident we should have reached Vicksburg in two days.

Given the garb we had to wear, we weren't so sure we would "fit in" with a crowd at a Miss Mississippi Pageant. We would certainly feel out of place. Packed in the bottom of our knapsacks, each of us had one spare clean shirt, reserved for special occasions. The shirt would be worn with faded, patched, beat-up, cut-off jeans and (once) white tennies. We wore this combo only twice before—in St. Paul and in Fort Madison, Iowa. Back then, however, the shorts and shoes were in far better condition.

As we paddled down the seemingly endless Great River, we talked mostly of Vicksburg. All I knew of Vicksburg was that it was the site of a great battle fought there during the Civil War. Since the day was blistering, without a wisp of wind, I vowed then and there that the first thing I would purchase in Vicksburg would be an umbrella. There had to be a way to mount it on the gunnel and thwart to provide some shade. It seemed Lou could handle the sun and heat far better than I could. I think I did enough complaining for the both of us.

Until just south of Memphis, with weather permitting, our daily dress was minimal. Shorts and a black bra. Black, so it wouldn't show the grime, even though washed. Later, we found it necessary at times to don light sleeveless shirts. I even found that to be hot, so I cut the collar off my shirt. Our denim shorts were always soaked with sweat. Hundred-degree days were not uncommon. While impending storms were our greatest fear, heat, sun, and humidity were our greatest adversity.

Early in the afternoon, we heard on our radio that a severe storm, which included tornado warnings, was on the way. That was all we needed. As fast as we could, we headed for the west shore. We had to find shelter quickly. As far as we could see in both directions, the riverbank presented an unwelcoming appearance. It didn't gradually slope to the river. Instead, it was a high perpendicular bank, with tree stumps protruding from it, left over from floods. It actually looked as if someone had taken a chainsaw and cut all the trees, even the bank itself. There just wasn't anywhere to go ashore.

This was a dilemma we had never before faced. As we sat in the canoe trying to figure out what to do, we heard a strange sounding horn. Looking out to the main river channel, a boat of the kind we'd never seen before, was coming toward us, seemingly at full speed. As it got nearer, we were able to read the words on its side: U.S. COAST GUARD! They, too, were looking for shelter. Later, we found out they were also on the lookout for us. From our time in St. Paul to this day, the Coast Guard cutters were nearly always aware of our whereabouts. In the mid-Mississippi, the lockmasters, we were told, notified the Coast Guard of our passing through their locks, or of our failure to appear when we should have. This was all news to us. How nice, though, to be looked after.

After a very short dialogue, we were taken aboard. The canoe was lashed tightly to the deck. With ropes at least three inches in circumference, the cutter was tied to tree stumps on shore. We three were escorted to the engine room below deck. It was determined to be the safest place for us.

We had barely entered the engine room, when a man on a upper deck calmly announced, "It's acoming!" I guesss we weren't the only ones who referred to a tornado as an "it," not a he or she as for a hurricane. There are just too many tornadoes to give each one a name. Inside the engine room, with a steel sliding door, we could hear the terrifying noise—a sound we had heard all too often. It was very much like the sound of a train. Hearing its approach, the engine room door was opened just a small crack so we could take a look. It was crossing the river west to east about a hundred yards north of us. Its immediate location wasn't hard to discern as the sky was packed with trees, branches, dirt, and other debris. As it churned across the river, it actually sucked water right out of the river. We were close witness to the devastating and awesome power of a tornado. So far, we had never been in the direct path of a tornado. As in the past, we received very strong winds and a good amount of flying debris. This time we could actually see it, while other times we had our heads buried in the sand and only heard its terrifying sound. This was a fast one. It didn't hang around as they sometimes do.

After it passed came a torrential downpour, a heavy, fat, cold rain. Even so, we were ordered to leave the cutter. Regulations did not allow us on the cutter since the danger was past. In the midst of the downpour, the canoe was put over the side. Lou and I took turns sponging water while the canoe was loaded with our gear and with Stinky, who came aboard last and was quickly tucked under the tarp. The rain lasted only a short time, but it came at us from all directions. The icy rain had only one blessing. It cooled us off.

Towards evening, after paddling several miles and seeing nothing on shore except tree stumps and steep banks, we finally found a sandbar suitable for a campsite. Another "fully filled" day had passed.

CHAPTER 38

The Encounter

THE NEXT MORNING, WE were up with the sun. We wanted to be in Vicksburg by mid-afternoon the next day. We had found that by getting up with the sun or even before, we would have several hours of paddling without the intense heat that was sure to arrive by 10 A.M. To our total disbelief, the whole day of paddling went by without incident. This was a rarity. Late that afternoon, we again camped on the west shore of the river. We most often camped on the west shore when possible, as it gave us more protection from storms that usually came from the west or southwest.

That evening, as we were preparing supper, a wind of some force sprang up. Since it came from the north, we paid little attention. In fact, we welcomed it, since it gave us some relief from the heat of the day. Stinky was lying in the shade of the tent, when without warning he took off for the river shore, about forty yards from our campsite. Much to our surprise and dismay, two bandy-legged men were getting out of their john boat that was pulled onto the shore. Both of us went to meet them. It was important that we keep them together and away from our camp—better yet, keep them off the sandbar. In the past, visitors always called to us to let us know of their presence, and in most cases, asked permission to land. There was something sneaky about these two. Neither of us liked the looks of them.

They had a small motor on the boat. We suspected that they had not used it as they approached our camp. If it hadn't been for Stinky's alertness they might have reached our campsite without our seeing or hearing them.

We hadn't expected any visitors in this remote area, especially since there were no small river towns or cities in the vicinity. Our unsavory visitors were small, skinny men, their faces covered with days-old whiskers. Their chin whiskers were saturated with "snoose juice," a nauseating sight and smell. They were missing teeth and they were filthy. It looked as if their clothing hadn't been washed in weeks.

I thought, "Oh God, what have we got here for visitors, and how are we going to get rid of them without creating a bigger problem for ourselves?" They began asking questions of us. They were the usual questions from visitors: "Where are you from?" "Where are you going?" and as always, "Where did you get the cat?" Trying to stay calm, we answered them the best we could, as it was quite difficult to understand them.

They had very deep southern accents along with a slurred, sluggish drawl. We, from northern Wisconsin, were not accustomed to this kind of speech. The last question we understood all too well! "Do you want company?" This question put us on full alert! Very firmly, we told them we didn't need or want company. We didn't *ask* them to leave, instead *told* them to leave. To our astonishment, they got in their boat and left without argument. But this had us wondering; there was something about their manner that we didn't trust.

The entire conversation during our belated supper dwelt on our unwanted, grubby intruders, and our distrust of them. It, too, was apparent that we didn't need a watch dog. We had a very dependable "watch cat." After supper, Lou got water from the river for dishes. She didn't see any sign of the men on the river or shore as far as she could see to the south, which was the direction they had gone when leaving. We believed they had gone back to wherever they had come from.

We hadn't even finished doing dishes, when they were back! Again they were out of their boat and on shore before Lou was able to react. Meanwhile, I went quickly to the tent and got both our guns and tucked them into my back jeans pockets and went to join her.

What I saw was very disturbing. Lou had sat on a large driftwood log. The two men were sitting on each side of her. To this day, I still don't know why she decided to sit on the log. *Now* what to do? Just to be on the safe side, I kept my distance from them. After a few words were exchanged, I asked Lou to come over to me, that I had something to ask her. She got up and came without interference from the men, even though they rose to their feet as she walked toward me. I wished they had stayed sitting.

As Lou stood next to me, I "palmed" a gun to her behind her back. It was too soon to let them know that we *each* had a loaded gun. As we stood there side by side, we again told them to leave. We didn't want them anywhere near us or our campsite. They, in return, assumed a stride position, hands on their hips, and saying without words, "Try to make us!" Their physically belligerent attitude struck a note of fear in both of us, but we didn't dare let them even suspect we were the least bit afraid of them.

We were about fifteen feet away from them. How I wished it was even further! But maybe it was just as well. The closer we were, the better they could see the guns that we suddenly pointed directly at them. Their hands dropped from their hips. They both had a look of total disbelief. One of them still held his stride position. I knew then, we had to mean business. I shot into the sand between the man's feet and told him the next one would be just a little higher if they didn't "git." In only moments, they literally jumped into their boat and rowed downriver as fast as they could. Either the motor didn't work or they didn't take the time to start it. We never saw them again! Even so, that night we weren't so sure. We made preparations in the event they should show up a third time.

We collected a large pile of driftwood, including some good-size logs, enough to keep a bright fire going all night. Neither of us went to bed. We took turns sleeping while sitting up, staying awake and on guard, and keeping the fire burning. Since we couldn't see into the dark, we depended also on Stinky's hearing, which was far better than ours. As he took turns sitting on our lap, we watched for "ear perks." His ears would tell us if there was anything unusual going on outside the radius of the fire's light. After what seemed like an extra long night, daylight finally came. Even then, we were still on the watch for the two men. Never before did we have visitors such as these two "river rats."

It wasn't long before Lou discovered that she had a very irritating condition. From her feet to her knees, hundreds of sand fleas had burrowed under her skin. Her legs and feet were so swollen and red, her skin took on a shine. Her feet were so swollen, she couldn't wear her tennies. The only medications we had to reduce the constant itching were calamine lotion and rubbing alcohol. Lou was a sound sleeper, and as a result she was an excellent target for the fleas. I couldn't sleep that night, even when it was my turn. In fact, I don't believe I slept more than four or five hours a night the entire trip. When I felt a slight tickling on my legs and feet, I would brush away what I thought were mosquitoes, which were constant companions. I didn't know that fleas were doing the tickling.

Later in the day, since our home doctoring didn't seem to improve her flea problem, we decided that she should see a doctor in Vicksburg, where we hoped to be the next day. The next day couldn't come soon enough. She was miserable from the fleas and anxious for relief. I was miserable from the sun, and eager to buy an umbrella!

CHAPTER 39

Vicksburg Antics

T HE NEXT DAY, AFTER a lot of paddling, we arrived at Vicksburg. We left the main river channel and entered the harbor waterway. It was called the Yazoo Division Canal. A canal it was—narrow, and deep with revetments on both sides for miles. After about an hour of paddling, we saw a large, old paddlewheel boat anchored on the canal shore. In all the miles we had traveled, it was the first paddle wheeler we had seen in the water and we guessed it to be in working order, since there were crewmen on its decks. We couldn't see the city of Vicksburg, as there was a high cement sea wall between the canal and the city. The wall was some distance from the river itself. At this time, the river was at normal level. The land between the river and the sea wall was nothing but mud, planks, weeds, and shacks. The people who lived on the river and canal side of the sea wall did so at their own risk. When the floods came in spring they were most likely flooded out. After the floods receded, the people just shoveled the mud out of their hovels and moved back in. In most cases, planks had to be walked to go to and from their little shacks. They lived there as squatters. In our estimation, these living conditions were intolerable for humans, even for animals.

Pulling in next to the paddle wheeler, we were able to get directions to place a phone call to a J.C. member. After a short wait, a young man came to welcome us to Vicksburg. He made arrangements for us to leave the canoe and most of our belongings on the deck of the paddle wheeler. No worry, all would be well cared for during our stay. Only our knapsacks and Stinky were taken with us to a hotel. When he saw Stinky, he had a look of total disbelief on his face! During the ride to the hotel, we told him all about Stinky and how we found him hitchhiking in northern Minnesota. He was somewhat concerned about Stinky. He wasn't sure what kind of reception a cat would receive at the hotel. The hotel personnel may not want him as a guest. He also didn't know of any J.C. member who might care for him during our stay. And even if he did, we weren't so sure we wanted Stinky separated from us for an extended period of time. The wheels were turning in both of our heads. If Stinky was rejected as a hotel guest, we had to come up with a plan.

We decided not to attempt to hide Stinky. If necessary, we could do that later. As we entered the hotel, I held Stinky in my arms. No one could miss seeing him. When the desk clerk saw him, she was at a loss for words. Finally, as we were registering, we were bluntly told NO CATS or any other animals were allowed in the hotel. It was also obvious she was very upset to see a *cat* in "her" hotel.

We told her that the young man with us would take the cat to his home. I'm sure this came as a complete surprise to him, as he knew nothing of our plan. This was the first time Stinky had been refused accommodations. The woman let us finish registering and gave us the keys to our second-floor room. The registering and keys were an important part of our plan.

We both went with the young J.C. man back to his car. We made room in my knapsack for Stinky by stuffing some of my stuff into Lou's knapsack. We tucked Stinky in and gave him directions on proper behavior. We tied down the cover flap. He'd been in a knapsack many times before, but always allowed to have his head out. Not this time! We just hoped he'd stay put, not wiggle, especially not meow. As we reentered the hotel and headed for the nearest elevator, the desk clerk was watching us. No CAT did she *see* or *hear*! So far so good! Much to our relief, an elevator came quickly and no one was in it.

We got Stinky into our room without any problems. But then a whole *new* problem arose, a Stinky situation we hadn't thought about. We didn't have a sandbox for him. Where was he to do "his thing?" So we hatched another plan! Again, all for Stinky's well-being. While Lou was taking her second shower, I stepped out onto the balcony area that encircled the entire second floor. One could see the hotel lobby from this vantage point. There were a lot of people in the lobby, but only a few on the balcony.

Like the people on the balcony, I too just strolled here and there— all the while looking for sand-filled cigarette urns. Since the sand in the urns was only inches deep, Stinky would need sand from several. With Stinky's tin cup, and feeling like a "thief in the day," I covertly removed sand from four urns. The cigarette butts, matches, and chewed gum were left in the urns. I hoped no one had seen my thievery. After all, it was only sand. If anyone did see me, they probably thought I was just some nut and let it go at that. Even so, I was still apprehensive of being caught and questioned by a hotel employee. That could lead to the discovery of the unwanted guest.

With all the nonchalance I could muster, I returned to our room with the precious sand. I had collected enough to last Stinky for at least thirty-six hours, which was about how long we would be in Vicksburg. Stinky was in the shower, playing with the dripping water from the showerhead. Surely he missed the opportunity to go wading, which was an everyday caper. I poured about a cup of sand into the corner of the stall. Only seconds passed before he did his thing. I directed the showerhead onto the sand and washed it down the drain. Voila! No evidence was left of a cat being in the shower. Plan #2 worked.

On the first day at the hotel, we took no fewer than three showers each. It felt so good to be clean and cool after weeks of heat, sand, and plain ole dirt. The more showers I took, the less I thought about an umbrella. The sun had become a distant memory. Lou saw a doctor about her flea problem. The doctor prescribed a salve that would more or less suffocate the little buggers. It must have been *less*, as it was several days before she had any relief from the itching.

That evening, it came to mind that we could run into another perplexing situation regarding the hiding of Stinky, that being the hotel's cleaning woman. After talking it over, we came to the conclusion that there were no options. There was no way we could hide Stinky. Plan #3 was formed. It would be a real gamble! Its outcome would depend on the attitude and compassion of the cleaning lady. We would not be devious about Stinky's presence. Instead, when she came, we would let Stinky be in full view, and hope for the best.

The following morning, the expected knock came. Immediately, we knew it was the cleaning lady! When she entered our room, Stinky was sleeping in the middle of a bed. When he heard the door close, he woke, gave himself a mighty stretch, and then just sat there giving the woman a good looking over. Never before had he been so aloof with strangers. His being so standoffish sure wasn't helping his cause. The look on the woman's face almost defies description, except to say it was a look of uncertainty. Am I seeing what I think I'm seeing? A *live cat*, here in the hotel? Gaining her composure, her first words were questions: How did you get *that* cat in here? Is it your cat? Is it house broken? Don't you know it's against hotel rules to have a cat in your room? Does the manager know? On and on she went with her tirade.

When her sputtering about the cat came to an end, she gave us a questioning look, waiting for a response from us. Lou asked her to sit and then proceeded to explain about Stinky, and how he came to be where he was. As soon as she sat, Stinky parked himself on her lap. I thought, "Good for him." Unknowingly, he was pleading his case. His unexpected act turned the odds in our favor. She assured us she wouldn't tell "one soul," and even passed on some complimentary remarks about Stinky. Problem #3 solved. All was "tight and ship-shape" in room 210.

In the afternoon, we dressed for the J.C. party. Dressing meant wearing the only clothes we had for the event. Cut-off jeans, knit shirts, and our only pair of beat-up tennis shoes. Some dress for a party! To say the least, we felt somewhat out of place. As we guessed, everyone else was dressed to the hilt. The young women vying for the Miss Mississippi crown were superbly dressed. As it turned out, how we were dressed didn't matter one iota. Everyone seemed to know who we were and how it came to be that we were at the party. True "Southern hospitality" was accorded us by everyone. Many of the city's dignitaries were present, including the mayor.

Food and drink were abundant all afternoon. Smoked catfish and goat, along with various kinds of entertainments. In spite of the fact that Mississippi was a dry state, we were offered bottles of Coca Cola spiked with liquor. Guess where there's a will there's a way!

Returning to the hotel we found Stinky hiding under a bedspread. He never like being alone and always found a place to hide.

The next morning, while Lou was showering, I stepped out into the hall overlooking the lobby. Since it was very early, no one else was in sight, except for a custodian who was cleaning the cigarette urns. As I watched him, he still hadn't reached the empty urns, but it wouldn't be long before he would. I just had to stay where I was, as I wondered what his reaction would be when he came upon the empty ones.

As he approached the first and second empty urns, all he did was shake his head in wonder. The third urn was nearer to me, and I could hear him muttering under his breath, and all the while shaking his head.

At the fourth urn, which was next to me, his grumbling reached its peak! Clearly, he was reaching a point of infuriation. Trying to show sincere curiosity, without a hint of humor in my voice, I asked him what seemed to be the problem? He said he couldn't figure out where all the sand went. "Why would anyone take sand out of urns? If it's for a joke, it isn't to me! Now, I have to refill them!" He was very confused.

Again, trying desperately not to laugh, I wholeheartedly agreed with him. "I can't imagine either why anyone would want to take sand. Maybe to plant flowers?"

"You can't plant flowers in sand," was his only response. Turning away, I retreated to our room, just a-grinning. He walked away mumbling to himself, madder than a cat on a hot tin roof.

CHAPTER 40

Sand and Muck Storm

By EARLY MORNING WE were packed and ready to leave the hotel. Stinky was again secretly tucked into my knapsack. And while Lou checked us out of the hotel, out the door we two went! Not even at the last moment did we want anyone to know we'd had a cat in the hotel.

A waiting car took us back to the river and our home away from home—the canoe. Our stay in Vicksburg was unforgettable. Especially the party, the numerous clean water showers, and the tour of the Vicksburg Battlefield, which was most impressive. After a hundred years some of the cannons mounted on their mobile carriages could still be seen. Evidence of hand-dug battle trenches were still very visible. Many monuments to the military forces of the various Northern states that fought the Battle of Vicksburg are on display. One of them is a monument to Wisconsin, an almost life-size rearing horse with an *empty* saddle.

The river map told us we had 360 miles to go to reach New Orleans. That meant a good week or more to reach our goal. Toward noon, after a few hours of paddling, I again began to yearn for the umbrella I failed to buy. The day and a half spent at the hotel sort of made me forget about the blazing sun. At the same time it was exhilarating to be back in the canoe. We reveled in the total freedom—no rules, no strict time schedule, no appointments, and best of all, not having to be properly dressed. If we wished to be just in shorts and a bra, we could do so without feeling immodest or shameful.

Late that afternoon, we made camp for the night. It was apparent that Stinky had missed the river and the sandbars. Moments after he was out of the canoe, he made one beeline for the river. He spent the next half-hour wading and puttering in the water. He surely must have thought this was much more fun that being stuck in a hotel room. He was back in an environment he had known since kittenhood.

When the tent was pitched, we discovered that we weren't on a "for-real" sandbar. Instead it was a very hard and dry mud flat with only a few inches of sand concealing the dried mud underneath. This was the first time we had camped on a bar such as this. However, we thought nothing much of it, except we were able to anchor the tent stakes firmly. No sagging tent this night.

After a couple of weeks, it was clear that Stinky was misnamed. "Digger" or "Wader" would have fit his personality far better. Whenever on shore, digging and wading were his greatest passions. Some of the holes he dug were so large and deep he could hide in them. On this bar, however, he didn't do much digging. As soon as he reached the dried muck, he would try in another place. Finally after a number of attempts he gave up. He was one very baffled cat! After being confined in the canoe most of the day, digging and wading was his way of expending his pent-up energy.

Every sandbar we camped on, from southern Minnesota to New Orleans, was left with numerous kitten diggings, by none other than Stinky. He always left his mark, even though each would probably be obliterated within days—but never erased from my memory.

I believe the evenings (except for the ever-present mosquitoes) were the most enjoyable. The sun was down, the intense heat went away, and we were another day closer to our destination. And we had time to play with Stinky, just relax, and ponder the next day. It was a time of pure contentment, a time of actually enjoying the scenic beauty of the river.

A short time after we hit the cots, we could hear thunder in the far distance. I guessed we were due for a storm, or at the very least some rain, as it hadn't rained for a few days. When going into the tent for the night, we had taken only our knapsacks, since we didn't expect rain. When we heard the thunder, however, we brought into the tent items that would suffer water damage outside. We emptied the metal cooler and set out to capture the rainwater that was now sure to come. Fresh water was always a precious commodity. We also brought the canoe up to the tent, overturned it, and secured the motor and life preservers underneath. We then felt that we were ready for anything the weather might bring us. How wrong we were!

While we preparing for whatever was coming, the thunder grew in volume and frequency. Occasionally a ghostly apparition of the moon broke through the swiftly moving black, chunky clouds. Strangely, there wasn't one wisp of ground wind. Since Stinky didn't much like thunder and lightning, we kept him in the tent while Lou and I watched and listened to the storm advance. When multitudinous streaks of lightning appeared, seeming almost to leapfrog each other, it was time to retire to the tent. Both of us had developed a profound fear and respect of lightning.

All too soon, the pitter-pat of raindrops were bouncing off the tent roof. It was the beginning of twenty-four hours of steady rain. As early morning neared, we became aware that the tent walls were drooping. The guy lines were slacking, causing the tent to sag.

When we stepped out of the tent at daybreak we found ourselves more than ankle-deep in black gummy slime. It clung to our feet like glue. The entire "not-for-real" sandbar was nothing but many inches of deep black muck. We then realized that we had chosen the wrong campsite. The hard, dried muck had soaked up every drop of water that fell. Not one bead of sand was left. All was pounded in the muck by the buckets of rain that fell. Our once picturesque sandbar had become a sea of malodorous muck! We spent most of the morning slogging through it.

We moved the overflowing cooler next to the tent door so we could wash the muck off our feet and legs before entering the tent—and there went our highly prized, bacteria-free water. Stinky couldn't possibly be put out into this muck to perform his personal duties. From sorry past experience he had become *very* wary of muck. In two or three steps he would have become stuck up to his belly and unable to move. We were able to scrounge some partially dry sand from under the tent floor and put it in a corner of the tent on tinfoil. Stinky knew immediately it was for him. The tent looked as if it were ready to collapse into the muck at any time.

For the next hour, we gave our full attention to the tent. Even though it didn't look much like a tent anymore, we had to keep it from caving in. It was the only dry and muck-free shelter we had. The stakes that we had driven into the hard muck were now so loose they could be pulled free with a finger. But the stakes were the keys to keeping the tent upright, since the roof guy lines were attached to them. After scrounging around some more, we were able to find some heavy water-soaked pieces of driftwood. We pushed these into the muck next to the stakes in an attempt to keep them firmly anchored. By the time the project was finished, and in spite of continuous rain, the muck covered our arms and legs. Our feet looked almost twice their size because of the clinging muck. We were both one sorry, smelly sight. If it didn't rain too much more, we believed the tent might survive in an upright position.

The rain continued without interruption all day, and we were forced to spend the day confined to the not-so-good-looking tent. Again all our meals were cooked on the camp stove. We spent most of the time observing the condition of the tent roof. In between, we played cards and entertained Stinky, all the while wondering when the rain would come to an end. I think Stinky knew what was happening outside. If we could smell the stench of the muck, he could too, only more so. He never even tried to leave the tent. Apparently he was perfectly content to be where he was.

Sometime during the night the rain came to a sudden halt. Unbelievably, the tent still stood!

At daybreak, we stepped out of the tent, onto what could best be described as a small island in a sea of muck. What we saw was a total shocker! It was as though the atmospheric powers had handed out everything there was to give us. This was an absolutely new twist in the predictability of the fury of the elements. In the beginning, the campsite was in a *sea of muck*. After more than twenty-four hours of unrelenting rain it had become a *giant ocean of muck*.

The sun was just beginning to make its appearance. Shining with an intense brilliance, it foretold of a very hot day to come. The business of breaking camp was almost overwhelming. It would have to be done according to our immediate needs. First was the canoe. Usually, when we broke camp, we would just carry everything to the river and park it on shore, then load it all at one time into the canoe. This day there was no place to park *anything*.

The overturned canoe's bow and stern, and even the gunnels, had sunk into the muck. Because of the suction, turning over the canoe was no easy task. When we finally did it, we found the preservers and motor almost muck free. The sinking of the canoe had prevented most of the rain from seeping under it. Camp was dismantled. We loaded our gear into the canoe piece by piece. Stinky was the first item to be loaded, instead of last. It was the first and *last* time we camped on a not-for-real sandbar. It was a little late in the game, but after that, we inspected each campsite thoroughly before making camp.

As we left "muck camp," which we had named it, we realized that we had traveled just a few miles short of two thousand. Never before, or after, did we have a campsite like this one. As the saying goes, "Chalk it up to experience." Had we paid closer attention to the river map, we could have avoided all the trials and tribulations of dealing with the muck. The map showed that our site was nothing more than a muck bar, well camouflaged by a small amount of sand. But it had looked so inviting!

At mid-morning we were on our way downriver. A fair amount of muck went with us, and would stay with us for several days—a constant reminder of our inattentiveness.

CHAPTER 41

Roast Turkey Buzzard

SEVERAL MILES DOWNRIVER FROM the muck camp, we saw three people on shore, jumping up and down and frantically waving at us. It appeared that they needed help. At the same time we didn't want to court trouble. The situation was akin to picking up unknown hitchhikers. As we paddled toward them, Lou got out the field glasses. The jumping up and downers were three young boys, who we later learned were on a four-day rafting trip. Their destination was Natchez, Mississippi.

We had barely gotten out of the canoe when they, all talking at once, related a story of trials and tribulations far worse than the ones we had in dealing with the muck.

Early that morning, their raft had hit a large, partially submerged deadhead near shore. The strong current overturned their small and poorly constructed raft. In seeing it, I wouldn't have tried going even a mile on it. Their entire food supply and some of their equipment was lost to the river. They did hang on to a .22 single-shot rifle. It truly was a tale of near disaster. One or all of them could easily have lost their lives.

As we walked to what could loosely be called a campsite, we saw a carcass of some kind skewered on a stick, roasting over a campfire. The smell of scorched and burning feathers was overpowering. The kids informed us that the odor came from a turkey buzzard they had shot for food. It was obvious that they had never cleaned so much as a chicken, let alone a turkey buzzard. Just the sight and smell of it was enough to turn our stomachs. They weren't the most careful of cooks, as the body of the bird was scorched black as pitch. They didn't even take the time to remove the normally featherless red head and neck, which protruded from one end of the skewer away from the scorching fire, allowing these parts to retain their original red color. Adding even more color to the scene, thick, dark blood was dripping from the bird's large, sharp beak, making it look even more repugnant!

I couldn't believe they intended to eat the horrible, smelly bird, as they were far from starving. Their food was lost only a few hours before.

There were only two reasons for "maybe" eating the buzzard: The first being curiosity—what would it taste like? The second, all three boys were probably trying to emulate the fictional Huck Finn. I don't recall if Twain's Huck Finn ate or tried to eat a turkey buzzard or not. It was apparent the boys were going to include the bird in their menu since it was the only so-called "food" they had.

Years ago, I myself, as a kid and even an adult, tried and ate various kinds of wildlife while on camping and canoe trips: chipmunk, muskrat, crow, red squirrel, clams, leopard frog legs, and crayfish, all of which are very edible if properly prepared. Fish-eating herons are a no-no! Today, they are also a protected species. We did it primarily for the novelty.

If the boys did finally try to eat the buzzard, it very likely would be very tough with a strong fishy flavor. Since it was a carrion-eater, it probably fed on dead fish along the river's shore and in the sloughs. Dead fish and animals were not few in number along the Mississippi.

Before leaving the modern Huck Finns, we gave them a few food items, including canned meat, potatoes, and powered milk. Last but not least, salt and pepper to season the buzzard.

We never learned where they had started their rafting trip, or if and when they reached Natchez. They had only fifteen miles to go, and with poling and paddling, they could conceivably do it in a day and a half. I like to believe that they made it. From our brief encounter, they seemed to be three boys with determination and a sense of adventure—both ingredients necessary for success. Even now, many years later, I wonder whether they ate the buzzard. I have my doubts!

CHAPTER 42

A Polluted River

AFTER ABOUT FOUR HOURS we approached Natchez. The river was filled with heavy boat traffic going in all directions, as was the churning water. The city's river shore was entirely industrial, which accounted for the large amount of boat and barge traffic.

Since we hadn't used the motor since Vicksburg, and it had to some extent been exposed to the elements at the muck camp, we wondered whether it would run or even start. After a few pulls on the starter rope, much to our surprise, it popped right off. With all the headaches we'd had with it in the past, and because it didn't have a name—which any car I had owned always had—we dubbed it the "Motor From Hell." Jokingly, I thought it might have heard us name it and decided to behave itself. We didn't laugh for long. After only a few minutes it just plain died. We checked the gas tank. It was empty!

The reserve gas can which we had forgotten to fill at Vicksburg was only a fourth full. We hadn't planned to stop at Natchez, but our need for gas forced us to change our minds. We never used the last few ounces from the reserve can. There was always a small amount of sand in the bottom and we didn't want it in the engine.

After a time of frenetic maneuvering amongst every species of watercraft imaginable, we found some "safe-space" which allowed us to paddle toward several barges tied to a revetment. Tying the canoe to one of them, Lou was delegated to find a phone to call for gas. After a few calls she found a gas station that offered to bring gas to us. It turned out to be somewhat expensive, but we had no other choice, since we still had three large cities to pass, including much of New Orleans.

For many miles the river had been tortuous. Now in addition, it also became narrower and deeper. It wouldn't be long and we would be encountering ocean-going freighters, among which we would find a whole new sense of smallness. I had the feeling of floating in a peanut shell when we encountered a vessel thousands of times our size and weight.

From St. Paul, all the way south to New Orleans, the terrain bordering the Great River gradually changed. The further south we paddled, the less wildlife we saw. In the upper Mississippi, wildlife was abundant. In the state of Mississippi, I once saw a small herd of whitetail deer. Other than that, I cannot recall seeing or hearing the croak of a frog or the quack of a duck, not so much as a turtle swimming or sunning its self on a sandbar. The immense pollution of the river precluded all wildlife. Gone too, or nearly so, are the fresh-water clams, because of pollution or over-harvesting to supply the button factories that once were in so many cities and towns along the river's route. Gone is the clear running water, gone are millions of edible freshwater fish.

Over the last two centuries, this once beautiful and pristine river has become a sewer for human waste, garbage, junk, and factory residue. Anything no longer needed or useable was and still is pushed, piped, or thrown into the river. The river has become a graveyard for cars, tires, batteries, TVs, stoves, refrigerators, and any other unwanted item. Name it, and in all likelihood it can be found somewhere in the river—out of sight, out of mind.

In addition, tons and tons of farm fertilizers and pesticides are washed into the river during every rainstorm and during spring flood-ing. Much of it eventually winds up in the delta area where the Mississippi enters into the Gulf of Mexico. The devastating impact of the fertilizers is especially apparent in this area, where a lack of oxygen has endangered sea life. The affected area is growing larger each year, threatening the livelihoods of those who depend on fish and shrimp.

Small rivers and creeks that we saw emptying into the Mississippi often didn't have a tree, weed, or a wisp of grass growing on their shores. This was the result of industrial pollution from towns and cities near the river.

There was one creek we attempted to paddle upstream. There was a little town only minutes away from the river, and we thought we could get groceries and fresh water there. We hadn't gone but twenty yards and found ourselves in milky-white water with the texture of soup. Not one live tree, bush, weed, or blade of grass was to be seen. Even the poison ivy was dead. Everything on either side of the creek, for almost as far as we could see, was dead. I had the feeling of being in a for-eign world. An inconceivably ugly and dreadful world. We made a quick turnaround. We didn't need food and water all that bad. The little creek left an impression that I will never forget. Later we learned that the small town housed a glass factory. All the residue from the manufacture of glass was pumped into the creek. In short order, it flowed into the Mississippi.

After seeing and smelling the pollution of the river, it's amazing that *any* fish are able to survive. I can only assume that the many dead fish we saw were the victims of pollution. Thanks to the turkey buzzard and other carrion feeders, most of the dead are soon eaten. If mosquitoes can be called wildlife, they were certainly not an endangered species along the entire length of the river. They are so plentiful in Minnesota, they are jokingly referred to as the "State Bird." Though we never caught one glimpse of a rattler of cottonmouth, I don't believe they are endangered, as we saw many "wiggles" in the sand, telling of their presence.

I often wonder what the early Native Americans, explorers, trappers, and settlers would think of the Father of Waters if they were to see it today. It has become a very valuable river to the cities along its shore, to industry, to the moving of freight, and to recreation. Even so, the unnecessary abuse it has endured over the centuries is certainly NOT praiseworthy.

CHAPTER 43

Donaldsonville

In a little more than three days we arrived at Baton Rouge without incident, except for one drenching, cold-water squall, during which time we collected fresh water and took a much needed rain shower without leaving the canoe. There was no danger of anyone seeing us stark naked, as the rain came in such a heavy downpour we couldn't even see the shore, which was only a short distance away. Happily the squall lasted just long enough for our showers and still gave us time to sponge the water from the canoe.

The squall was unusual in that it came without any warning and the rain was icy cold. We were left shivering, even though the temperature was nearly a hundred. It was still raining buckets when we got back into our already wet clothes. We donned ponchos in an effort to get warm. Minutes after the squall passed we began to sweat. Off came the ponchos. It was an unfamiliar experience to shiver one moment and then sweat the next. By the time we reached Baton Rouge we and the canoe were all dried out.

We didn't stop at Baton Rouge. The city's entire shore was industrial for at least three miles. There were, however, a few things we needed in the line of food, since we had given away some to the boys. Because it would take a couple of hours to accomplish the shopping, we would eat what we had. It wouldn't be too many days until we would be at Donaldsonville, where a stop of several hours was planned. According to our calculations, it was fifty-six miles from Baton Rouge to Donaldsonville, where we hoped to be by early morning the next day. After leaving Baton Rouge we paddled another twenty miles before making camp in early evening.

In another twenty-five or thirty miles we would be in Donaldsonville. We hoped to be there by mid-morning, but that meant having a good river current and getting underway no later than 4 A.M. Getting up early, but with an absence of a good river current, didn't do the trick. It was shortly after high noon when we arrived, which we found to be the worst time of day to tie up and go ashore.

After more than two thousand miles, it was obvious we were beginning to show wear and tear along with our clothing, tent, canoe, and just about everything we owned. Any item that was once white in color was now a dirty grey. Stinky was one exception, unscathed from his river adventure. As always, he was full of mischief and dauntless spirit. He was having the time of his life. A time, I think, many kittens and cats would have given their left paw for. Our "butts" were also beginning to rebel. They were getting somewhat fed up with sitting on the hard fiberglass seats most every day and all day. Much of the "gung-ho" spirit we'd had in the beginning had been lost, somewhere, to the river and the elements.

As we neared the city's waterfront proper, the river traffic was more than abundant. Eventually, we found a place to go ashore. We figured it to be safe and far enough away from the coming and going of towboats, barges, freighters, cruisers, and pontoons. No canoes were on the scene except ours. After leaving the upper Mississippi, we never saw another canoe. In the south, we were asked more than once what kind of boat we had. Canoes must have been a rare mode of travel in the South.

The space we chose for a landing was near a ferryboat landing. The ferry was busy unloading and loading vehicles for crossing the river. Lou was again delegated to make the phone calls to our parents, who were to have mailed the suitcases (ones we had packed more than two months earlier) to the Sheraton Charles hotel in New Orleans. We would be in need of clothing other than the grubby duds we now wore. She also called the hotel, telling them of our expected arrival date. Arrangements had been made earlier with the hotel management for accommodations upon our arrival. Much to our astonishment and appreciation, we were to be their guests. GRATIS!!

Lou was gone for quite some time as she had a difficult time finding a pay phone and a grocery store near the waterfront. Shortly after she left for the errands, Stinky and I just sat in the canoe watching the ferry unload and load the many vehicles waiting their turn, and chatting with some of the locals.

All of a sudden and without warning, I could feel and see the bow of the canoe move upward. I was in total disbelief as to what was happening. I thought, "What the hell is going on?" Was I really seeing and feeling what I thought, or was the sun at last getting to me? When the bow of the canoe was about three feet above the surface of the river, for some unknown reason, I looked toward the ferryboat. A large steel cable leading from the ferry passed underneath the canoe to its anchoring site on shore. A young man was hand cranking a winch to which the cable was attached. What was happening was not in my imagination! Over all the noise, I began screaming as loud as I could and at the same time waving my arms to get his attention. Thankfully, he heard and saw what was occurring and dropped the winch handle. Immediately the cable slackened, and the canoe dropped back into the river with such force it was close to being sunk because of the shifting of weight. Up until that time much of our gear in the bow had slid toward the stern where I was sitting. The stern was only inches from taking on water. Never in my wildest dreams did I ever expect that we could be dumped by a ferryboat cable!

After the cable incident, the winch man directed me to a safer site. It was a move of only a few yards from where the cable was anchored to shore. I made the distance a little further just to be on the safe side. By the time Lou returned, I had put all the gear back to its proper place. She did wonder why I had moved the canoe, and why there was water in it. After I told her of the harrowing experience, we came to realize it could have been a disaster for us, for the canoe, and for the completion of our trip. The canoe could have been severely damaged or even dumped. If dumped, everything we had that didn't float would not have been retrievable because of the great depth of the river at that particular location.

CHAPTER 44

River Hitchhiking

By mid-afternoon Donaldsonville was behind us. Late in the afternoon we chose a small sandbar surrounded by small trees for a campsite. We wouldn't have to cut and haul branches for shade, since it was all ready-made. Some of the trees were large enough to hold a cat. We knew they would be enticing to Stinky, and so we decided to keep him in his harness with the long leash. A cat in a tree, one that might refuse to come down, we didn't need! Every little while, to keep him occupied, we moved him to a new area to investigate. He most enjoyed being near the river so he could puddle around in the water. Playing and wading in the river was seventh heaven for him. In the Deep South, maybe he missed the frogs, crayfish, and minnows he had tried to capture as a tiny kitten.

That evening, since we had only seventy-five miles to go to reach New Orleans, we unwisely disposed of items we thought to be no longer needed and considered surplus weight. Most of the dirty, gray towels, which had become rags and didn't even resemble towels anymore, were burned along with some of our clothing items that were almost unwearable. Far from the river's shore, we dug a hole, along with Stinky's help. Extra pots, pans, water containers, metal cooler, and other supposedly now-dispensable items were buried. Since no rain or severe weather was predicted for a few days, our ponchos were also burned. A small pile of what we believed to be excess food was stashed in among the trees, for any animal that might find it.

When our disposal project was finished, we estimated the canoe was lightened by at least fifty pounds. The only water container we kept was a GI water can, whose cap was slightly damaged and was no longer leak-proof. Of all the containers we had, it was in the best condition, but it was not a rain catcher since the opening on top was too small.

That night, when we went to bed, we felt very satisfied. We'd lightened the canoe, which was our main purpose. Also, when we reached New Orleans, we wouldn't be burdened with unneeded or worn clothing and gear that would have to be transported to the hotel and then back to Wisconsin.

Sometime during the night, I heard the sound of rain! I must be dreaming. It can't be! The weather forecaster had said no rain was predicted for a few days. It seemed like the more I listened, the heavier it came down. By morning it was still coming down in sheets, with no indication of letting up. The sky was a solid blanket of gray. It looked as if it could be an all-day rain—and it was! We passed the morning in the tent by telling each other how senseless we were to be in such a rush to "unload." Especially the ponchos, food, and the water containers which we crushed before they were buried. Now we were without any means of collecting any of the rain that was steadily falling, and we had nothing to store it in for future use, since the GI can was full.

It appeared we could be caught in a bind because of our failure to think ahead. At noon we decided to pack up and be on our way. Rain or no rain, ponchos or no ponchos, we had to get some miles behind us. We could feel the loss of fifty pounds in the canoe as we made our way downriver. Luckily it was a warm rain and, as usual, the day was warm, too. Wind, lightning, and thunder were absent, which made our paddling in the rain quite pleasant. Best of all we didn't have to deal with the glare and heat of the sun. By late afternoon we had covered only about fifteen miles, as much of our time was devoted to sponging water out of the canoe instead of paddling.

Eventually we found a sandbar for camp. We left Stinky in the canoe, under the tarp, while we pitched the tent. As soon as it was up, we put him on shore. He did his thing, and then made one fast bee-line for the tent. He despised rain with a passion. We could never quite understand why. He liked to swim, wade, and even lie in a rain runoff. Maybe because as a kitten, before we found him, he had been rained on too many times and didn't like the rain hitting his head. Or maybe cats just don't like to be rained on.

By the next morning, the rain had stopped. In its place, we had a heavy, thick fog, so thick you could almost cut it with a knife. Even though the sun hadn't penetrated the fog, it was sticky hot. Everything we had left was either waterlogged or damp. We had only the clothes we had worn the day before. We had wrung the water out of them the night before, but they were still soaking wet when we crawled into them in the morning.

As we were preparing for breakfast we found, much to our cha-grin, that the GI water can had tipped over during the night. We had made the mistake of putting the can on a slight slope. The rain had washed away the sand from under the can, causing it to tip over. Only a few cups of water remained, the rest having leaked out via the damaged cap. We would save the few remaining cups for drinking and brushing teeth. Coffee that morning was made from river water. It looked and smelled like coffee, but was far from tasting like coffee!

By the time we were ready to leave the sandbar, the sun was making an effort to break through the dense fog. It wasn't a matter of if, but rather *when*. The "when" came about 6 A.M. With the intense humidity it was nothing less than sticky hot without a breath of wind. A short time later I cut the collar off my one and only "river shirt," hoping it might make me feel cooler. At the bottom of our knapsacks, we each still had one pair of long jeans and one knit shirt reserved for special occasions. The last special occasion was to be in New Orleans, so they escaped a scissors attack even though we were in dire need of a pair of cut-off jeans. To wear our special clothes while still on the river was unthinkable. Also, we wanted to wear reasonably clean clothes when we arrived, and not smell too much like river tramps—which we knew we did!

Still about sixty miles from New Orleans, we realized that we had miscalculated our arrival date. In the South, we weren't able to paddle as many miles in a day as we could in the North. Some days we found it next to impossible to spend eight to ten hours a day on the river with the blistering sun, along with ever-increasingly tired backs, arms, and butts. We considered thirty miles of progress to be a good day. By comparison, we paddled forty to fifty miles in an eight or ten-hour day in northern Minnesota and Wisconsin. Once, and only once, we paddled nearly eighty miles in one day when the Mississippi had a great drop in elevation. The fewer miles paddled can also be attributed to increasing fatigue. We were just about "used up," but at the same time refused to give in to the Great River. We'd gone too far to give up so close to our ultimate destination.

When noon arrived, we had used up the few remaining cups of fresh water. During our rest at noon we began calculating our position—the number of miles to go, the lack of drinking water, and not much food. Any river water we drank would have to be boiled as we had lost the little bottle of purifying tablets somewhere along the river. Buying food anywhere was out of the question. The little towns we passed were not riverbank towns, instead being some distance from the river, and there were large revetments between them and the river. After talking over our situation, we found only one solution—something we had never done before. We would camp early and then try to flag down a passing towboat and ask for help. It would have to be a towboat that wasn't pushing any barges. A tow pushing barges was not likely to stop.

At 4 P.M. we called it quits for the day and made camp. While setting it up, we also set our little plan into motion. We kept a lookout for a passing towboat. We were lucky the main river channel was only about two hundred yards from our side of the river.

Most of the tows we saw were pushing barges. Two were going south. Even though that was the direction we were heading, we didn't attempt to flag them down. If a southbound tow should happen to stop, whichever one of us who went to meet it would have to motor upriver back to camp. And as we had learned, our little motor was not all that dependable. Neither of us wanted to have to paddle upriver if the motor decided not to run. Our hopes were pinned on northbound traffic. But

114

by early evening, we had seen only one northbound tow, that one pushing barges.

The canoe, water can, one paddle, and the motor on its mount were left on shore. Since the motor had sat in the rain for a day and a half, we decided to test it. On the second pull, the starter rope came out of the engine head in shreds. What more could possibly go wrong? We didn't have a replacement, or any kind of rope or cord that might even come close in size to the original. The little "motor from hell" had breathed its last breath. Now, even if we were able to flag down a tow-boat, it was highly unlikely they would have a rope of the kind we needed. We took the mount off the canoe and left the motor in the bow for ballast.

It was now apparent that we would have to paddle, and paddle quickly, to any approaching towboat. In addition, we wouldn't have a motor to help us through the expected sixteen miles of very heavy river traffic in the city of New Orleans before we reached Napoleon Street Landing, where we had been told to land.

We flipped a coin and Lou won the first turn in trying to flag down a towboat. She paddled toward the first northbound towboat without barges, waving her life preserver. No Luck! Either they didn't see her or decided not to stop. Since it was so late in the day, we would have our supper and try again in the morning.

We found a small pothole that still held enough rain water to make a pot of coffee. The pothole also had a number of small worm-like insects wiggling around in the water. To me, they looked like recently hatched mosquito larvae. By straining the water through a paper towel we were able to have coffee without the "whatever" insects. Our supper was the old standby—pancakes, canned bacon, dried fruit, and the coffee. We had to eat all the bacon or it would spoil. As usual, we had no ice or even a metal cooler. Stinky had his full share and more, especially of bacon. Breakfast would be the same menu, minus the bacon and coffee. If everything went right for us, we could still arrive in New Orleans the day after next.

The next morning we were up at daybreak. We had to stop a tow-boat today! In reality I felt like I was hitchhiking for just a short ride. We had to have, at the very least, some fresh, pure drinking water. Boiled river water just wouldn't do. Lou had an allergy that required a shot every three days. She had only one metal syringe and the needle had to be boiled before each use. Forty years ago, disposable syringes were almost unheard of. The bottle of medication she had was supposed to be refrigerated, but never was. Apparently it didn't matter, as the shots did what they were supposed to do.

Between daylight and mid-morning, only three towboats passed, all going north. Three times one us paddled out to try to get their attention. Waving a life preserver and even flashing a small mirror did nothing. We began to think that they surely saw us, but maybe believed that we were just two boys playing hanky-panky. We decided that we had to find some way to let the towboats know were not boys clowning around. How to do it was the big question. We were silent for a while, each with our own thoughts. After a bit, I suggested to Lou that when the next towboat shows up, I was going to paddle out in only my black bra and shorts—in short, in almost nothing. Then they would know for certain that we were not mischievous boys, but rather two women in need of help. I had done some road hitchhiking in the past and even some river hitching—but never half-dressed. I have to admit, I felt utterly ridiculous.

The wait wasn't long before we saw a towboat heading north at a pretty good clip. Now I was to execute the plan. As I paddled out, I thought: "Hey! Dorie, do you really want to go through with this?" Right after, another thought came to mind. "Chalk it up to experience." It will be something you'll always remember. Nothing was a truer thought! When I was parallel with the towboat and about seventy-five yards away, I took off my shirt and waved it along with the life preserver. In a heartbeat, the towboat slowed and came to a stop. Much to my delight, our little scheme worked.

Putting my shirt back on, I paddled the last fifty yards to the towboat. A crew member handed me a rope to tie the canoe, and I was helped on board. The towboat started up and continued on upriver, which I knew it would do. They had a schedule to keep. Within three or four miles of travel upriver, I explained our problems and needs. The men of the crew that I met were both courteous and curious. I guessed they were curious because of my appearance and my sudden arrival on their boat. I was asked all the whys? wheres? when? and how comes?

Telling them of Stinky and how he adapted to river life intrigued them more than anything else. They were somewhat reluctant to believe that a kitten growing into cathood had traveled more than two thousand miles in a *canoe,* of all things! The captain said he'd heard many a story in his life on the river, but never one about a canoe and cat. I was trying to be as brief as possible, as I knew the longer we talked the further I'd have to paddle back to Lou and Stinky. As we talked, the towboat went around a bend in the river and the campsite could no longer be seen. Lou, I guessed, was probably wondering how long it would be before I would be back.

The captain and crew were more than generous and kind. Again, a towboat crew came to the rescue of two damsels in distress. And these were the boats that we initially cursed under our breath and sometimes out loud. Our water can was filled. I was given three meals of food: canned vegetables, eggs, bread, cured sausage, a can of beef stew, and even some butter. I couldn't remember the last time we had had butter on the river. I told them about our motor problem, but they were unable to supply any kind of rope or cord to replace the old one.

They also offered a number of safety tips for when we reached New Orleans. The first was: Stay OUT of the main river channel, as it would be teeming with towboats, barges, ocean-going freighters, and numerous large pleasure craft. Our canoe would be an oddity, and it might attract interest which could be troublesome for us. This would be especially true of the pleasure craft. From a past experience, we were well aware of this possibility. New Orleans was the largest port on the river, and one of the most dangerous for small craft. I was advised that we should take our time, and be on the alert for wayward river traffic. Many of the freighters, being foreign, were not familiar with the port or its regulations. Added to that, many of the crews could not read or speak English. As the crew bid me luck and farewell, I found myself back in the canoe with the precious cargo.

With the help of a good river current, I made it back to our campsite in no time at all. Lou had taken the tent down. Most of the gear we had left was piled near the shore. Stinky sat next to the pile, as he always knew when we were breaking camp. He probably wondered what had happened to his home, the canoe. We had a quick lunch, compliments of the towboat crew. Then we packed the canoe. We put

Stinky in first, so that he could have time to find a comfortable spot by himself. The "motor from hell," now very dead, was put in the center of the canoe, under everything else.

We left the sandbar shortly after noon. Our goal was to paddle at least fifteen miles, which would leave us with about forty-five miles to the outskirts of New Orleans. According to the river map, we made our goal of fifteen miles that day. Our supper that night almost seemed like a banquet. Thanks to the towboat crew, we had food of a kind we hadn't seen in some time.

That evening we determined that we'd have to go at least thirty miles the next day. Then we would be in striking distance of the city the following morning. It was important that we entered the port city during full daylight, so that we could see and be seen. Being run over by another craft was not in our plans. For the next two days, the word of the day was prudence.

CHAPTER 45

The Last Lap

U P AT THE BREAK of day, we realized that we would have only one more morning on the river after this one. But that would only happen if we had a good day this day. Even though it was hot and muggy, the weather was beautiful. Not one cloud, a crystal blue sky, and best of all, no rain or storms in the forecast. The day couldn't be better for what we hoped would be our last full day on the river.

At noon we found a small sandbar with some scrubby underbrush. There was just enough to give us some much-needed shade. We spent an hour soaking up the shade while having lunch. Stinky found some damp sand in the shade and dug himself a nice big hole to lie in. He found that was another way to cool off other than lying in the water. Another fifteen miles and we would look for a place to camp for the night. It would be our last night on the river.

The entire day went unusually well for all three of us. Stinky, still the "Commander in Chief," spent a short time on the bow, his favorite perch, surveying the scenery as well as other craft which had begun to increase in number. We stayed close to shore where the water was too shallow for anything other than a canoe or rowboat. In doing this, it required us to be on the watch for underwater bank protection which, if struck, could lead to problems—a damaged canoe, a dumping, or both. After Stinky had had enough of the scenery and sun, he whiled away the afternoon under the tarp, lying on the bottom of the canoe and enjoying the coolness from the river.

The day was probably one of the most relaxing we'd had in quite some time. Our talk dwelt on our days on the river. We recalled events of the days long gone, including of how family and friends thought we were losing our minds, or had already lost them for even considering paddling the Mississippi River. Some remarks actually bolstered our resolve. We were out to prove our sanity, and that being women was not a valid reason for our not challenging the "Father of Waters."

We talked also of our concern for Stinky. We never informed the hotel management in New Orleans of our secret companion. The hotel in Vicksburg would not allow him as a bonafide guest. We wondered whether the Sheraton Charles Hotel in New Orleans would accept him. If they didn't, what would we do with him? That was the big question. We didn't want to smuggle him into a hotel again, since we would be staying at the hotel for at least three days before returning to Wisconsin. And since we would be there gratis it wouldn't be fair for us to smuggle him in. To us, boarding him at veterinarian's was out of the question. He had never been in a cage in his life, and he'd probably not eat, as he didn't like cat food. We felt it would be too great of an environmental transition for him. If it came to smuggling him again, we would just do what we had to do.

As we neared New Orleans, the map indicated more and more revetments, levees, contraction works, and bank protection, and we could see more of it, too. Sandbars suitable for a camp were few and far between. It was now late afternoon and we had paddled nearly fifteen miles.

It was only six miles or so to the Napoleon Street Landing. Now we really had a vexing situation. Should we make a run for the landing in spite of the lateness of the day, or try to find a place to camp for night and make it to the landing the next day? We decided to sprint to the landing.

Chapter 46

New Orleans!

Before we reached the landing site, we had to find a place to wash up and change into our "special occasion" clothes. Just a tiny sandbar would do. We dreaded the thought of changing into long jeans, but the sun was almost down and it wouldn't be as hot as during midday. Had we camped for the night, we would have arrived in mid-morning.

About five miles north of the proposed destination in the city, we found a wee bit of sand surrounded by all sorts of gunk. The levees were approximately a hundred yards from the river's shore, which gave us the opportunity to pull ashore. This was the first piece of sand we'd seen in quite some time.

Stinky woke the minute the canoe bumped the shore. As Lou got out of the canoe and pulled it further onto the sand spit, he parked himself on the bow seat. As I got out, I picked him up and set him on shore. I figured he must be ready to do his "duty," which he quickly did without even bothering to dig a hole or cover it up. Much to our astonishment, he jumped right back into the canoe and sat on the bow seat the entire time we stayed on the spit of sand. Apparently all the gunk in the area was not to his liking. He didn't want any part of it. We didn't like it, either, as there was a foul, noxious odor. To Stinky it must have smelled much stronger, and possibly reminded him of his past encounters with muck.

With some of the last of the clean drinking water, we washed and fixed our hair, which was no longer really fixable. Even though we both had our hair cut short and wore (formerly white) sailor-type caps with the brims pulled down, our hair was dried out and brittle. The river's water was just about the filthiest we'd seen, with patches of oil slick floating most everywhere on the river's surface.

After we had washed our hair, we used most of the same water to scrub the balance of our bodies. If we had used river water, we probably would have been dirtier after than before. We changed into our only long, clean jeans and shirts. By now the sun was down and gone. Even so, the long jeans and knit shirt felt miserably sticky and hot! I guess the changing of clothes and our washing and primping didn't make much difference, as we were still an oddity as we entered the hotel that night.

Our grooming and scrubbing had taken only a short time, but by then it was nearly dark. By then, too, all three of us had pangs of hunger. Stinky rarely meowed, but this evening he let us know he was also hungry and thirsty. We had only biscuits and butter to eat, along with the last of the drinkable water. Stinky ate and drank all he wanted. He was especially fond of butter, and probably ate the biscuit just because it had butter on it and because he was one very hungry cat, much like the day we found him as a kitten.

After finishing our meager supper in the canoe, we paddled back into the river. It was now dark. Because of the lights from boats, freighters, factories, landings, and buoy markers, we had ample light to see where we were going. We hugged the shore away from the buoy markers that indicated the main river channel, thinking that maybe this was the best time after all to enter the city. It turned out to be so. The river traffic wasn't nearly as heavy as we thought it would be.

That evening, I threw my raggedy, collarless, colorless shirt into the river. "Good-bye shirt! You served me well!" I had worn it nearly every day from Keokuk, Iowa, to this night. It was a yellow and white checked shirt when it began its journey. Now it was a dirty gray and dark yellow. As I watched it float away and finally sink out of sight, I felt as if I were throwing away an indispensable part of myself. But the shirt was no longer wearable, and it smelled of the river and mold, like everything else, including the two of us. Stinky was the only one of us who didn't smell bad. With his everyday wading, lying in rain rills whenever possible, and constant grooming, he was always immaculate. I do not recall that he ever shed. We never found his hair on our cots where he slept at night, or on our clothing. I believe it was because of his being outside his entire life.

As we neared the Napoleon Street Landing, which was marked on the river map as 92.6 Inner Harbor Navigation Canal #2, I began to realize that our river odyssey was very near its end. Emotionally, I was aware of a feeling of both happiness and sadness. We had an experience and adventure few people will know, and one I'll NEVER forget! To this day, forty years later, whenever I see the Great River, I can still visualize a little red canoe, a kitten on the bow, and two paddlers. Memories, many fond and some not so fond, come flooding back.

About nine o'clock that night, we entered the canal. A couple of hundred yards into it, we found a well-lit wharf. Hoping we were at the proper location, we tied up to a deck ring. Stinky and I stayed in the canoe while Lou went hunting for a telephone to call the hotel to tell them we had finally arrived and where we had docked. Even though there were many other wharves nearby, by pure happenstance we had picked the right one. While waiting for transportation to the hotel, we unloaded the canoe and for the last time pulled it from the river. The canoe and all our baggage were piled on the wharf. Stinky, thinking it was a good place to take a catnap, topped it off.

Shortly thereafter, a big, black limousine appeared on the wharf. Even though we were the only two people to be seen on any of the wharves, we didn't suspect it was for us. In moments, four men, all with big smiles on their faces, approached us. We could hardly believe they had come in a limousine just for us. Two young, well-dressed men were the emissaries from the hotel. With them were a reporter and a photographer from the *New Orleans States Item*.

The attention we received was far more than we had anticipated. The picture-taking session of us, Stinky, and the men from the hotel, and the interview, were longer than any we had had in other communities. As usual, Stinky was the center of attention, and he deserved to be, as he was the unifying force that helped us complete our venture. The saying: "Two is company, three is a crowd," was not true in our case. Stinky was our company. He added laughter, and a state of contentment to our sometimes near "I-give-up" days.

Since the men from the hotel knew nothing of Stinky being a part of the crew, many of the questions asked of us were about him. At the first opportunity, I asked the one and only question we had: Will Stinky be a welcome guest at the hotel? We were somewhat fearful of the answer, for if it was no, what would we do with him? Much to our relief, the response was affirmative. Arrangements were made to leave the canoe on the wharf until the next afternoon, when more pictures would be taken of us in the canoe, and in the daylight, dressed in our usual river clothes. Only a short while before, we had thought we had pulled the canoe out of the river for the last time, and now it looked as if we would do it one more time.

The following day the canoe would be shipped by rail back to the Core Craft Canoe Company in Bemidji, Minnesota. The hotel management would make all of the arrangements for shipping the canoe. With the attention and assistance we were receiving, we couldn't help but feel we were celebrities. When we left the wharf, nothing less than a limo could have handled all of our baggage, a cat, and six people.

CHAPTER 47

The Hotel

AFTER A RIDE OF some distance, we arrived at the Sheraton Charles Hotel. Our limousine was one of many waiting in line to drive up the hotel's main entrance. We noticed that the people entering the hotel were all young and in formal dress, the men in tuxedos and the women in floor-length gowns. When we entered the main lobby, we felt like we stuck out like sore thumbs. Our attire was a far cry from formal. Here we were, dressed like tramps! Beat up tennis shoes, jeans, sunbleached shirts, knapsacks on our backs. Stinky's tin cup hung from a clip on my knapsack. This time, however, Stinky didn't have to be hidden in my knapsack; I held him in my arms for all to see. Before we could even reach the desk to register, the music that a small band was playing came to a sudden halt. We stopped in our tracks as well. Now all of the people in the spacious lobby had turned to look us over from top to bottom. They appeared to be spellbound by the sight of us. Some, holding their hand over their mouths, began to whisper to each other. I could only imagine what they might be saying. Maybe like ... "WHO in the hell are they?" ... "What in the world are THEY doing here?" . . . "They look like moneyless tramps!" . . . Why did the hotel let THEM in? And with a CAT, of all things!?"

As we registered at the desk, out of the corner of my eye, I could see that we were still being scrutinized, especially by the young women. Later we learned that the doings in the lobby were a part of the "coming out" ritual for the debutantes of New Orleans.

While we were registering, the porters brought in all of our gear and camping equipment, which they stored in the baggage room. Fortunately, it was a large room as we still, even after ditching some stuff a few days earlier, had a good amount left. We were also told that the baggage room was to be Stinky's room as well. We weren't too happy about this, but it was better than nothing. At least he was with us in the hotel. The baggage man prepared a box of sand for him. Of all things, it was the kind of sand used in cigarette urns. And this time it didn't have to be swiped. Stinky would be allowed to have full freedom of the room. With most of our stuff in the room, he was among familiar things, except that we would be missing. We had become so attached to him, it was hard for us to leave him there, even for only a few days.

We were escorted to a small suite of two rooms. One was a bedroom, the other a sitting room with TV, a bowl of fruit, and a vase of flowers. The fruit and flowers were compliments of the hotel.

It was nearly midnight by the time our knapsacks were unpacked and our showering finished. The showering was heaven itself, as we hadn't been in a shower since Vicksburg. How good it felt to be cool and CLEAN! We then went out for a midnight snack. Considering how hungry we were, we figured Stinky must be hungry, too, and so we each saved some of our meal to take back to the hotel for his supper.

The waitress gave us a funny look when we asked for an extra napkin for the saved food. We told her it was for our cat, but from the look on her face, I don't think she believed a word of it. She probably thought we were saving it for another meal for ourselves. Still wearing some of our old river clothes, we did, I had to admit, look destitute. When we returned to the hotel, we found Stinky sound asleep on the baggage attendant's lap. When he heard our voices, he awoke instantly, and he made no bones about showing how much he missed us.

We fed him his supper, and gave him a tin cup full of water. After drinking a small amount, he used most of the rest of it to wet his forepaws and groom himself. During our prolonged visit with him and the attendant, Stinky's purr motor ran the loudest it ever had. It seemed as if he couldn't stop it. With Stinky stuck in the baggage room, we made every effort after that to visit and play with him several times a day. The baggage attendants had taken a liking to him, so we knew he was in good hands. Each morning and evening, we harnessed him and took him for a walk outside. He didn't like the hard, hot sidewalks.

The next day, on Stinky's first morning walk, and we in our "river clothes," because our suitcases hadn't yet arrived, many, many people would stop us and say, "Hey, you're the women and the CAT!" Unknown to us at the time, we had been the cover story in the early edition of the *New Orleans Edition* newspaper. Much to our surprise, and even embarrassment, some even wanted our autograph. I think we were recognized, more than anything else, because of Stinky being on a leash. He was the real celebrity, not Lou or I. I now sometimes marvel how he, a small cat, survived the rigors of the journey—the storms, tornadoes, heat, poisonous insects, muck traps, and the river itself. In addition, there were times he had to fend for himself. When we found him, he barely weighed a pound. By the time he returned with us to Wisconsin, he weighed in at eleven pounds, without eating one morsel of cat food. He had become one robust, healthy cat.

Every time we took Stinky for a walk during the three days in New Orleans, people approached us. Most of the questions they asked were about Stinky. Again, many people wanted him for their own, especially the children. Some even wanted to buy him. Of course, we refused all the offers. Stinky was going home with us.

On the morning of our second day in the city, the suitcases finally arrived. Now we could start looking presentable, like normal women. After being, for the most part, barefoot for over two months, our "heels" were less than comfortable to wear. For the next two days, we had nothing but sore feet.

Since we now had some decent clothing, the hotel management made an appointment for us with the mayor for that same afternoon. More pictures were taken as he presented each of us with "Keys to the City" and a document that stated that we were Honorary Citizens of

New Orleans. All of which we considered to be a great honor, since we felt we were, after all, just two nondescript school teachers who, with a lot of luck and help, managed to cope with the Great River on a summer's so-called *vacation*. The keys were small medals, shaped like a key, to be worn as a pendant. Now, forty years later, my key and document are still cherished treasures and mementos of the greatest adventure of my life.

During the morning of the third day, we went back to Napoleon Street for more picture-taking. This time the pictures were to be of us in the canoe, with the canoe in the river. This was certainly the last time the canoe was to be put in the river. When I think about it, the canoe, during our trip, was put into and pulled out of the river no less than three hundred times, an aspect that we never considered when we began the trip.

Late in the afternoon, my sister Marilyn and her husband Don arrived by car to take us back to Wisconsin. When they came into our room, my sister had a look of shock and wonder on her face, and for a moment was wordless. Being my sister, she could and would be honest with me. Her first thought and utterance was: "You two sure look like hell!" The remark wasn't far from the truth. We not only looked like it, but also physically felt like it. It was a very hot day, and we had put on our river-worn, cut-off jeans after the picture taking in the morning. We definitely looked like tramps.

We made plans to have dinner that evening at the Three Sisters, a fine restaurant in the French Quarter. My sister gently hinted that she hoped we would change our clothes, as they would be embarrassed to be seen with us, dressed as we were. We assured her we would change, even though our present outfits were familiar and made us feel much more comfortable. A few days later, on our way back to Wisconsin, we and Stinky would be an embarrassment many times.

The next day, the last full day in New Orleans, someone—I don't remember who (but it sure wasn't me)—got the idea to take a boat tour of the New Orleans harbor. I couldn't imagine in a "month of Sundays" that I would buy a ticket for a boat ride on the Mississippi, after being in a boat of sorts on the river for more than two months. But, buy I did! My sister and her husband did enjoy the tour. Lou and I just saw more of the same scenery we had seen before, except for a small aircraft carrier. After an hour of riding around the harbor, Lou and I were more than ready to go back to the hotel. The tour of the harbor had quickly filled our cup to overflowing of the river.

CHAPTER 48

Stinky's Wild Escapade

THAT EVENING, WHEN WE went to take Stinky for his last walk in the city, he pulled the biggest and most fantastically disordered caper of his young life. I always believed he had a clock in his head. This evening it was demonstrated, as he was ready and waiting for us in the baggage room. The minute the door was opened, he came flying out like he was shot from a cannon. Like a streak of lightning, off he ran through the lobby. Up, over, under, and on every piece of furniture in the place. We threw off our heels and took after him. Most of the women in the lobby were screaming their heads off. Stinky ran so fast I don't think they even knew it was just a busy, playful cat. He ran across one woman's lap and scared the wits out of her! She screamed, "Get that creature away from me!" She ended up standing on the chair. Other women began doing the same. The men in the lobby only laughed at Lou and me trying to catch our evasive cat.

The scene in the lobby was total bedlam as well as an embarrassing situation for us. Calling Stinky by name was to no avail, he was having the time of his life! During the chase, he would crouch down under or behind a piece of furniture and peer out at us, daring us to catch him. To Stinky, the whole episode was just fun and games. Finally, with some help from hotel staff, we got him cornered and were able to latch on to him. We were thankful that he was not a cat that ever bit or scratched, so no one was hurt during his wild prank.

We made apologies to all of the guests that Stinky had frightened. We explained about his unusual upbringing and promised that it would never happen again—especially since we all were checking out the next morning. None of the guests berated us for his behavior. In fact, some wanted to know more about him. One elderly man came to us with an amused expression on his face. He thought Stinky's run, with us in close pursuit, was "great entertainment" . . . It had "made his day!" Stinky sure put the finishing touches on our last day in New Orleans, as well. It seemed he was getting fed up with being kept confined to the baggage room. He was just itching for a good run, which he did accomplish. We got a good run, too, but it was not on our agenda.

CHAPTER 49

Finale

VERY EARLY IN THE morning of the sixth of August, we packed the car for the long ride home, back to Wisconsin. After all the baggage and gear were stuffed into the trunk and into every space available inside the car, very little room was left for four humans and a cat. Since the car didn't have air conditioning, we harnessed Stinky on a very short leash, as all of the windows had to be open. We couldn't risk his getting a notion to jump out of a window. Every once in a while on the entire trip home, someone would ask, "Who's got the string?"— meaning, who's hanging onto Stinky's leash? He was never in the same place two times in a row. Except for the driver, it took all three of us to keep track of his whereabouts.

Only once did we stop at a drive-in for a quick lunch. We made two or three stops for a leg stretch and gasoline. That evening after sixteen hours of driving, we found a motel on the outskirts of a small city whose name I no longer remember, except that it was about eight hundred miles north of New Orleans and just east of St. Louis, Missouri. Near the motel was a nice restaurant with a bar. For us it was a perfect place to spend the night. We four would rent two units, and smuggle Stinky in via my knapsack as we did in Vicksburg. We would leave him in the air-conditioned room while we went to the restaurant for a cold beer and supper. When Lou and I entered our room with our smuggled companion and shut the door, a small card was seen tacked to the back of the door. It was a notice of the kind I had never seen before, nor have I ever since. It read as follows:

128

PETS ARE WELCOME

They don't steal towels, bedding, or break furniture.

They don't have drunken brawls or uproarious parties.

They don't disrupt other guests with loud TV or radios.

P.S. Our back is a fenced area where your pet can

defecate and exercise. Please keep your pet leashed

when outside.

Thank you,

The Management.

How we came to be so lucky to have chosen this motel I'll never know. The short notice on the door was totally unexpected. It made our day, and Stinky's too. For the first time in days, he could get some exercise on real ground and not a sidewalk. Best of all, he could resume his habit of eating a little grass if he wished.

After Stinky's needs were met, we took our showers and dressed in our traveling clothes, which were none other than our cut-off jeans, faded shirts, and beat-up tennis shoes. By the time we were ready to leave our unit, Stinky, after spending all day in the car with no catnap, was sound asleep on one of the beds.

We were to meet Marilyn and Don at the bar. Since we arrived before they, we seated ourselves at the bar. The bartender took one glance at us and proceeded to shake his head in disbelief and wonder. Eventually he came to us with a quizzical smile as he asked for our order. When he returned, he quietly but bluntly asked us, "Where in the hell are you two from? It looks like you've had a rough time of it. I hope you have the money to pay for your beer."

We had begun to answer his questions when Marilyn and Don walked in. I could tell they really didn't approve of our dress, but Lou and I had been on the river too long to care.

After a short time, the bartender returned to where we were sitting. He apologized for his rude questions and became extremely talkative. Since we didn't have an opportunity earlier, we told him where we had been and why we looked as we did. Stinky, an integral part of our river odyssey, wasn't left out of the story. The mere mention of Stinky made him all ears. That was one cat he'd sure like to see. We told him we would be having breakfast at the restaurant the next morning, and that he could see Stinky then, if he wished. Much to our astonishment, we were allowed to bring Stinky into the restaurant.

The next morning at the appointed time, we four and Stinky went for breakfast. There weren't too many customers, but the few who were there took a double take when they saw us with Stinky walking in on his leash. A cat in a restaurant? But we were used to the stares. We had seen them before.

Last night's bartender was now the morning's waiter. Stinky, being on his best behavior, won a new admirer. When our breakfast was served, Stinky was given a small dish of scrambled eggs and chopped bacon. When we got our checks, Stinky's was separate from ours. His check said, "On the house." Once again, Stinky had won a new friend.

The second day on the road was almost an exact replica of the first. As we drove further north, it became cooler and less humid. The pleasant weather was something we hadn't felt in quite some time. Late in the afternoon we arrived at Madison, Wisconsin. Now we had only 200 miles to nearly complete the last segment of our trip home. My final destination was Medford, Wisconsin. Lou and Stinky, too (as it turned out), still had another 125 miles to reach Spooner, Wisconsin, their final destination.

Late that evening, when we entered my parents' home, they, too, had a look of disbelief at the sight of us. Later that night, my mother commented, "Now I'll be able to sleep at night, and not have to wonder and worry where you are, or if you're alright." Her remark made me then realize how frustrating it must have been for her. It was something I had never thought of before this night. A number of years later, when I became a mother, myself, I could fully comprehend how it must have been for her. No matter how old your child or children are, a mother's caring never lessens.

Our parents weren't too surprised that we brought a cat home with us on this vacation. The previous summer we had brought home two part-wolf Eskimo puppies from Alaska. There's nothing like bringing home a live puppy or cat as a souvenir of a vacation.

Lucky for us, our parents never objected to our bringing home an addition to the family. The summer of 1959, Lou and I took a four-week trip by car to Alaska. Intending to see all we could see in the two weeks there, we flew from Fairbanks to Kotzebu, a small Eskimo village on the Bering Sea, north of the Arctic Circle. In the early part of June, there were many Eskimo puppies of all ages to be seen. For some reason or another we got it into our heads to buy a puppy each. We found five, three-week-old, almost pure white puppies housed in the bottom of a large oil barrel. An Eskimo woman, a neighbor of the puppies' owners, told us the pups were for sale. We could have any we wanted for two-fifty each. Figuring it to be a fair price, we picked out two little females, flew them to Fairbanks, and then drove by car back to Wisconsin. Getting those two tiny pups home in an MG sports car with no air-conditioning is another story.

Getting back to the river trek, that night when Lou called her parents, she received the devastating news that her Husky "Frosty" was apparently shot by some linemen, who had mistaken her to be a full-blooded wolf. Even if she had been all wolf, the shooting was illegal, since wolves were on the endangered species list. My Husky "Kamik" survived the summer and lived to be ten years old. Since a dog of this kind, unless raised with a cat, seems to have a built-in hatred of cats, we decided that Stinky would be safer at Lou's home than at mine. Had Frosty not been killed, my sister would have taken Stinky.

The following day I drove Lou and Stinky to Spooner. By now, Stinky must have been about five months old and still very much a kitten. Considering his traumatic early life, he had grown considerably. And since Lou's home was just outside the Spooner city limits, we thought it would be an ideal home for him.

On a weekend in mid-September, we went once again to Bemidji, the home of Paul Bunyan and the Blue Ox—this time, to personally thank the president of the Bemidji Boat Company for his generosity in providing us with a canoe. While packing the car at Spooner for the trip to Bemidji, Stinky followed us around like a trailer. Apparently he was ready for another car ride, so we took him with us. The people at the boat factory would probably like to meet the third member of the crew.

As we drove to Bemidji along Highway 2 in northern Wisconsin, we occasionally drove next to, crossed, or were in sight of the Mississippi River. Some of the sightings brought back memories. Grand Rapids, near where Stinky was found. Deer River, where we were lost in the tall grass swamp. Cass Lake, which we referred to as the "lake of near disaster." At the small town of Ball Club, the highway crossed over the river. Three months earlier we had paddled under that bridge. It felt somewhat strange to view familiar sites from the comfort and safety of a car instead of a canoe.

When we reached Bemidji, we had an all-afternoon visit with Dick Vogel, president of The Bemidji Boat Company. There, with some of his family and friends, we showed over a hundred colored slides of our trip. We had thought we were all finished with newspapers, reporters, and photographers, but much to our surprise two young men from the local paper were also there to interview us and see the slides. Stinky, as I suspected, occupied the limelight.

The canoe that was shipped back to Bemidji had arrived in good shape. It went on display the following spring at the Twin Cities annual boat show. For a number of years thereafter, it was displayed at the show, until the boat factory where it was stored burned to the ground, along with the canoe. For "doing" the river, the company gave each of us a new canoe.

As I write this book I regret that we didn't note the names and addresses of all the people who came to our aid and took us into their homes and aboard their boats for our comfort and safety. I also regret that we couldn't take pictures of storms or rough waters—but when the water was rough, we were too busy paddling and sponging water. At other times, taking pictures would have been inappropriate, such as in the logging camp that didn't want visitors, anyway. And at other times, I simply didn't think of how much I would have wanted pictures in years to come!

Chapter 50

The Demise of Stinky

Deer season that November proved to be extraordinary. Lou's mother, a deer hunter the same as Lou and I, insisted that Stinky go deer hunting, too. The weather was mild that hunting season, without a single flake of snow on the ground. Stinky, in harness and leashed, is the only kitten I have ever heard of going deer hunting. Lou's mother had him sitting on her lap each day at her deer stand. Since a cat's hearing is extremely sharp, Stinky alerted her to a number of deer before she heard or saw them. All she had do was watch his head and ears. Whenever he looked steadily, with his ears perked forward, she eventually saw the deer he heard coming. She didn't shoot any of the deer. It was more fun just watching them and Stinky, the "deer hunting kitten."

Stinky became an indoor-outdoor cat. In mid-January of 1961 he went outside one day and never returned. We never learned what happened to him, but there were a number of possibilities. He could have been killed by a dog or another male cat. Being so young and with little direct experience, might not have feared these two. He could have been run over by a car, caught in a trap and killed by the trapper. Being poisoned or shot was another possibility. I have always wondered how and where he met death.

Stinky was an integral part of our odyssey. Without him, it wouldn't have been the same. He added amusement and gaiety to our days on the river. In his known nine months of life, he had seen and experienced more than most cats do in a long lifetime. Even if he didn't know it, he negotiated the Father of Waters, saw ten different states, survived some harrowing times, and may have had some adventures we never knew about during the time he was with us. Putting the finishing touches to his short life, he went deer hunting. To me, he was a much-loved kitten who became very special in his very short life. I think we were the first women of record to "do" the river, and if not, I'm quite sure Stinky was the first and only kitten to do it. He is the one reason I made the effort to write this book. I believe his story of the river is worth telling.

Since I have lived for more than forty years within a hundred miles of the Mississippi, on occasion I see it, or cross over it on a bridge. Then my "mind's eye" reverts to a time long past: a little red canoe, we two, and Stinky perched on the bow, taking in the sights. Now, at age 74, with a bit of aging and wisdom, seeing the river from a different point of view is somewhat "goosepimpling." It almost seems like a dream that we "did the river" so long ago.

AFTERWORD

For those of you who might consider canoeing the Father of Waters, the following information may encourage or dissuade you.

Become experienced canoeists. Canoeing the Mississippi today could be more difficult and dangerous than it was in 1960. The river traffic is likely to be heavier and less forgiving. We practiced two summers in Canada, never knowing then that we would later challenge the Mississippi. The first summer, some locals we met gave us one short lesson on the finer points of canoeing. They (men) thought we were idiots to be in the wilderness of Lake of the Woods without any previous canoeing experience. In canoeing the river, we found at the very beginning that we were still novices. River canoeing is far different from lake canoeing. I would also suggest that you have some wilderness camping experience under your belt.

Expect to spend a few months in preparation for the venture—unless you already have a canoe, tent, and all the other necessary equipment. Make reservations in advance for your arrival at your ultimate destination, and arrange in advance for your return home, as well as that of your canoe and gear. You might want to contact civic groups along the river's route.

Today, there are more options for protection than the handguns we depended on. In 1960, mace and pepper spray were not available. If a handgun is still your choice, get a permit to carry one legally. Mace or pepper spray would be a valuable deterrent for skunks—much better than a gun.

Have a physical examination and a tetanus shot. If you have any medical problems, but none serious enough to prevent you from having one of the greatest adventures of your life, be sure to carry an adequate supply of medication, as well as a doctor's prescription for any drugs you might need along the way. A good first-aid kit is a must.

Acquire the most current maps (charts) of the river.

As a society, we are not as safe as we used to be, no matter where you are or what you're doing. In this day and age, if we were canoeing the river, we wouldn't find ourselves trusting nearly everyone we met. On the other hand, you may not find people as eager to help you when in a tight situation, because they don't trust *you*.

134

One other aspect has changed. In 1960 we were a novelty and a very rare sight on the Mississippi, especially having a kitten with us. We had invaded the "men or boys only" arena. Some people thought we'd never reach New Orleans simply because we were women. Today, girls and women have entered once forbidden arenas in many ways. We as women are no longer restricted to certain professions, or limited to specific sports or athletics. I suspect that there are more women making extensive canoe trips now than there were in 1960.

Many people do not consider a canoe to be a safe watercraft. I found it to be as safe as any other small craft. It is easier to maneuver in rough waters or rapids. Unlike other small boats, the bow is in the water and cannot be as easily up-ended by high winds, which I once experienced in a twelve-foot aluminum boat.

My choice of a canoe would be fiberglass, for a number of reasons. If it sustains any damage, you can repair it quickly and easily with a kit. During an electrical storm, fiberglass is safer than aluminum. And a fiberglass canoe makes little noise when in use.

Two extra paddles (which we didn't have) and a waterproof canoe cover are of utmost importance.

For personal needs, don't pack more than necessary. Forget the pillows; they are too bulky. An item of clothing can serve as a pillow. If you plan to start in northern Minnesota, have plenty of warm clothing and a sleeping bag. You will need a poncho or raincoat the entire distance. Make arrangements to meet someone in the Twin Cities of Minnesota, or shortly thereafter, for exchanging or adding clothing and gear.

There is plenty of good fishing to be had in northern Minnesota. We each had a casting rod and a few plugs. We tried trolling a floating plug, but found we could feel the drag of the bait, and it often got snagged. We soon discarded the idea of trolling. We never fished at day's end. We were just too tired after spending all day on the river, and the overwhelming masses of mosquitoes presented another deterrent. We dumped the fishing gear when we reached the Twin Cities.

In 1960, sun-block lotions were not available. We went through bottles of lotion and plain old suntan oil, but they provided no blocking, and the sun was tough on our skin. Be sure you're well stocked. Plenty of mosquito repellant is also a must.

Weather is not always conducive for making campfires. Have an alternate means of cooking. A one-unit LP gas stove is adequate. Flashlights, with extra batteries and bulbs, are necessary items. Even a small kerosene lantern can come in handy.

We used only one kind of soap, which was very versatile. Ivory liquid and bar was used for dishes, clothes, and personal bathing. It worked for everything, except our hair. When taking a bath in the river, we never had to hunt for the bar of soap, because it floated.

The Boy Scout motto is, "Be Prepared." When canoeing the Mississippi River, I suggest you add the words, FOR ANYTHING!

I might also suggest that you do what we didn't do: keep a daily journal. We did write notes on the maps from St. Paul to New Orleans. In northern Minnesota, nothing was noted, as we had only a road map to follow. Most of what I have written is from memory. It was the kind of experience one doesn't easily forget.

How much would a trip of this sort cost today? It would depend on the help you may or may not receive, how much traveling is necessary before and after the canoeing, and, how much equipment you may or not already have.

In 1960 there were no credit cards such as MasterCard and Visa. We had American Express checks in fifty-dollar denominations. We never carried more than fifty dollars cash on our persons. The American Express checks were kept in a waterproof container and stashed in the bottom of our knapsacks. Using one of the back straps, the knapsacks were strapped to the canoe's thwarts. We always kept them in the tent when we went ashore.

I estimate the plus two-month journey cost each of us about six hundred dollars. Today, it may very well be much more costly.

Should any of you decide to challenge the Great River, I wish you the best of luck for what may be the greatest adventure of your life. Be sure to drop me a card!